"Laugh-out-loud humor." —Diane Scharper, *The Washington Post*

"If you're tired of working but think retirement is only for the injured, the incontinent, or the rapper Jay-Z, *Early Bird* will be music to your lazy ears. . . . [Rothman's] encounters result in rapid-fire laughs."
—Paul Ulane, *Maxim*

"A very amusing and surprisingly tender tale. . . . This gentle, good-hearted memoir . . . shows us this particular early bird really gets the worm."
—*The Hartford Courant*

"Very sweet and very funny . . . Rothman allows the sadness that must, of course, attach itself to the end of our lives to seep through slowly, surely, and entirely without sentiment."
—Nick Hornby, author of *The Polysyllabic Spree, High Fidelity,* and *About a Boy*

"I'm so into Rodney Rothman. Imagine if your coolest friend retired in his late twenties, moved to Florida, and then wrote you about it in the most observant, sweet, yet unsentimental way. Rodney is one of those uniquely funny and human writers that belongs on your bookshelf next to the Eggers, Klostermans, and Sedarises. Don't be late to the buffet."
—Greg Behrendt,
coauthor of *He's Just Not That Into You*

"Hilarious." —*Newsweek*

Early Bird

Rodney Rothman

SIMON & SCHUSTER PAPERBACKS
NEW YORK LONDON TORONTO SYDNEY

SIMON & SCHUSTER PAPERBACKS
Rockefeller Center
1230 Avenue of the Americas
New York, NY 10020

Names and identifying characteristics of some individuals and locations in this book have been changed.

First Simon & Schuster paperback edition 2006

For information regarding special discounts for bulk purchases, please contact Simon & Schuster Special Sales at 1-800-456-6798 or business@simonandschuster.com.

Designed by Davina Mock

Manufactured in the United States of America

10 9 8 7 6 5 4 3 2 1

The Library of Congress has cataloged the hardcover edition as follows:
Rothman, Rodney.
Early bird : a memoir / Rodney Rothman
p. cm
1. Retirement communities—Florida—Humor. 2. Retirees—Florida—Humor. 3. Retirement—Humor. I. Title.
HQ1063.2.U6R68 2005
306.3'8'09759—dc22 2005042460

ISBN-13: 978-0-7432-4217-2
ISBN-10: 0-7432-4217-3
ISBN-13: 978-0-7432-7058-8 (Pbk.)
ISBN-10: 0-7432-7058-4 (Pbk.)

To my grandparents:

Avy and Samuel Rothman
Leonard and Helen Solomon

The tragedy of old age is not that one is old,
but that one is young.

—Oscar Wilde, *The Picture of Dorian Gray*

Part One

EARLY BIRD

I LOST MY JOB IN JANUARY. The television show I was working on was canceled. I've been raised to believe that losing your job is a bad thing, but I am more relieved than disappointed. I've been working seventy hours a week for the better part of a decade. I've spent more time in my office chair than I have in my bed. My wrists twitch. My back throbs. My butt hurts. When I close my eyes, I see a blinking keyboard cursor. I'm twenty-eight years old, and far too many of my memories involve me sitting in my office after midnight, tasting every quarter-filled coffee cup on my desk until I find the one that is still a little warm.

Now I'm off work and I don't care. I may not be a coal miner, but work is work, and I need to stop doing it for a while. I don't know what I want to do next. Everyone says I should make lists of what my priorities are and see where that takes me. It's nice sometimes to be told what to do. I try making lists of "important things," and "life goals," and "meaningful values." I take long walks, praying for epiphany. Epiphany does not come, so I get pizza instead.

Being unemployed makes everyone around you nervous. Nobody knows what to say to you. At parties and dinners, making small talk, you're always supposed to be *doing* something, or at least *up to* something. "So what are you *doing*? What are you *up to*?" they start to ask, once a few weeks have passed.

I tell them I'm "off work" or "taking time off," terms I've come to resent because they remind me that I'm supposed to be "on." Years ago, people would call this "taking a vacation," which had a nice, assertive ring to it, but nobody I know calls it that anymore. The first place I vacationed was Florida, to visit my grandparents. It blew my eight-year-old mind. The snowstorms and school-yard fights of my typical New York February were far away. My family rented a convertible and drove around as an actual family for once, listening to bad radio like Lionel Richie. But down in Florida, I learned, *Lionel Richie sounds good!* I'd get sunburned, and my grandmother would call it "healthy color." I would sleep on the world's only comfortable cot, listening to the ocean through the window screen, and my head would sing: *Hey! Jambo jumbo!*

"I'm Jewish," I say to myself one day. "I'll end up retired in Florida anyway. Why not get a head start and check it out?"

My friends say the whole plan sounds neurotic. My family agrees, and also wants to know if I have a date yet for my sister's wedding.

"This is what it is," I tell my friend Jill, who I met, of course, at work—where else do you meet people these days?—when I used to be a joke writer for David Letterman, and Jill was a segment producer. "I move down to Florida and test out retirement early. I get to relax in the only place I've ever actually been relaxed. And while I'm there, I get to see what retirement is like forty years before I get there. I get to see if working hard is worth it. Maybe I meet a bunch of wise elderly people who inspire me and I somehow figure out a way to write a book about it. I've read *Tuesdays with Morrie*. I know how it goes."

"You're kidding me," she says.

"Everything is so accelerated lately," I say. "Maybe I've crammed a lifelong career into seven years."

"Sweetie, you go insane when you're not working," she says. "You gotta go back to work."

"I don't," I explain to her. Instead of actually doing work I can at least tell people at parties, when they ask me what I'm doing, that I'm "writing a book." Then they will say, "Oh, wow, a book, that's great." I could drag it out for years.

Americans are surviving longer and longer these days. Between the Bronze Age and 1900—about 4,500 years—our life expectancy extended twenty-seven years. In the last hundred years, thanks to medical advancements and better home care, our life expectancy increased the same amount. Replacement body parts, the Human Genome Project. We're going to live a long time. I don't want to get ready for those final years the way I get ready for a dental cleaning, maniacally flossing for two days to make up for months of neglect, then acting surprised when the hygienist says my gums are infected. What's neurotic about being exceedingly prepared?

My first step is to somehow find a way to live in a retirement community. My grandfather tells me that it is unlikely I'll find one that will allow me to move in. Most Florida retirement communities have strict fifty-five-years-and-up policies. I ask him if any of his elderly friends have empty Florida condos I can squat in. I have always thought that my grandfather's wellspring of unconditional love is bottomless, but this request manages to scrape rock. He is nice enough, though, to set me up on a meeting with a New Jersey neighbor of his who keeps a condo in Boynton Beach, Florida. Unfortunately, she tells me, with a Dominican nurse sitting imposingly behind her like a bodyguard, that she is selling the condo any day now; it won't be available.

I join Roommate Finders of Florida for one hundred dollars. I tell them I want a roommate over the age of sixty-five. They don't seem troubled by the request. Perhaps that fact should have troubled me. A few days later, they call back and say they've found me a roommate in Boca Raton. Her name is Margaret. She is in her mid- to late sixties. She lives in Century Village, one of the largest, most famous retirement communities in the country. It caters mainly to lower-middle-class Jews from the Northeast. I've heard of it before. It's one of these fully loaded communities: swimming pools, tennis courts, a huge clubhouse full of meeting rooms and social events, and more than five thousand condominium units for retired people.

"One question," they ask. "Do you have a problem with cats or birds?"

"Not enough of one," I say.

The night before I leave Los Angeles for Florida, I throw myself a going away party at a tiki bar. A handful of my closest friends in the city show up. After two years here in Los Angeles, I'm still amazed by how few people I actually know well. It's not like it used to be, when we were in our early twenties and everyone would stay out late all the time. We'd all buy each other shots and then vomit together in the streets. Really great times. These days it seems like everyone is staying in; small dinner parties or just crashing out on the couch watching *Six Feet Under*. I wonder how much I'm really going to miss any of these people.

For my last night, though, we rage for a few hours like the

old days. People give me AmberVision glasses, adult diapers, "Sexy and Sixty" cuff links. We drink piña coladas. Naturally, there are many crude jokes made about me romancing old women. The next day on the plane, I'm glad I got drunk at my party and I'm glad I am hungover. It blunts the edge as my plane descends toward South Florida, as I wonder what the hell I am doing, looking out over the paisley landscape and beginning an early retirement.

EARLY MORNING IN CENTURY VILLAGE

Old people, they make young people scream.
Old people, they make young people lay down and die.

—Robyn Hitchcock

MANY OLD PEOPLE get up early, at around six in the morning. It's not because they need less sleep, as I'd been previously informed. It's most likely because they sleep less deeply, due to decreased levels of sleep hormones like melatonin. It's a gyp, really. You've made it to the time of your life when you can finally sleep in as late as you want, and now your body won't let you.

I've been forcing myself to get up early, like real retirees do. I walk outside at six-fifteen in the morning, and it couldn't feel more absurd. The sky above the greater Boca Raton area is still more black than blue. Outside, Century Village is full of elderly people already out for their day. They are moving at full speed. They are jogging, walking, swimming laps in the swimming pool, ambling around the tennis courts. At six-thirty in the morning, I have seen several men waxing their cars. They are wide awake; they are not sleep-waxing. Melatonin shortage doesn't begin to explain it.

I should have laid a little more groundwork before I came down here. I realize that now. Most people, when they retire, go someplace where they already know a lot of people. My grandparents, when they used to live here, settled near all their old friends from Queens. I remember when I used to come down and visit them here, they'd always go out of their way to make me feel comfortable and relaxed, and to introduce me to everyone.

"You remember Harris," they'd say, "from two floors below us in Rego Park?" Some guy I'd never seen before, with white chest hair sprouting out of his shirt, would swat me on the head. Then we'd all go play bingo together, or go down to the pool, or go out to Denny's. Great vacation memories. This was years before I realized that Denny's is a terrible restaurant.

But my grandparents don't live here anymore. Harris died. I underestimated how different it would be in South Florida without all those people. I think I half expected they'd still be here. I don't know any of the retirees anymore, and the only piece of small talk my groggy brain can come up with is: "Why are you waxing your car at six-fifteen in the damn morning?," which doesn't feel neighborly.

By late morning I end up trying to call someone back home. A family member or a friend. I just want to talk to someone who knows me. With the phone pressed up against my sweaty ear, I pace around the parking lot in front of my condominium, the only place where I can get halfway-decent reception. If I manage to get someone on the phone, he sounds stressed and busy, which cheers me up. It is a useful reminder of why I wanted to come down here to begin with.

"I can't talk," my friend Matt says, "I'm working." I hear

his fingers clacking on a keyboard. Matt works two jobs at once; he is on the payroll at one place and runs his own business at the same time.

"I think I made a terrible mistake," I say. "It's lonely here."

"I don't have time for this," he says. "Just talk to people," he says. "They're old. They're lonely too."

What was it in the fifties that caused retirees to begin moving, en masse, to Florida? It's been attributed to the advent of Social Security in 1935. Nothing like it had ever occurred before. Suddenly, elderly people had a guaranteed income. They were no longer forced to work until they couldn't, and then, if they were lucky, die in their children's house. They could choose how and where they wanted to grow old.

I wonder if any of the elderly people questioned the motives behind Social Security. Did they feel taken care of? Or did they feel like they were being pushed out of the workplace too soon? It's not as if anyone prized their wisdom and experience anymore. Old-timers knew how to milk a cow, or foxtrot; that didn't help Colgate sell more toothpaste. Georges Minois, in *History of Old Age,* writes that the elderly, "living in this world, felt they no longer belonged to it. The activities, attitudes and distractions of the young were forbidden to them."

Never before in human history had senior citizens decided to get up and move far away from everyone else, their families and hometowns. But that's what happened. At the age of sixty-five, they decided to become pilgrims and start a new colony. They went to Florida, and claimed their Shuffleboard Zion.

So I've been trying to approach the retired people here and start conversations with them. I force myself to walk up to them mid-wax. I just want to bite the bullet, and accelerate the process of adjusting to the retired life. It will pay off in forty years, when I'm far more ready for the transition than my friends and loved ones are.

Walking up to strange people is a terrifying prospect, even if they have friendly, wizened old faces like the people down here in Florida do. But I learn after a few attempts that most people around here are open to me. This is mainly because they assume that I am someone else's grandson.

"You look like Sybil. Are you Sybil's?" one says.

"Which Sybil?" says another. "Fourth floor or ground floor?"

"I'm not Sybil's," I say. "I'm here to try out retirement early."

"That's a good idea," they say. "Whose grandson are you?"

Once I convey that I'm nobody's grandson, the retirees tend to get cagey. "What are you selling, then?" they always ask, half joking and backing away. Young men who aren't anybody's grandson are probably scam artists trying to fleece the elderly out of their savings. I've seen the flyers around the community warning residents to "Report Salesmen and Unregistered Visitors to Security!!!!!!!"

So I usually tell them that I'm a professional writer. I tell them that I used to write jokes for David Letterman, and that always seems to placate them for a few minutes and open them up for a little conversation. I seem more like a vacationing professional and less like an off-putting weirdo who is living in their community for no discernible reason.

"So is retirement what you expected?" I ask them first. It's my icebreaker question.

"It's hard when you first get here," a man admits to me, as he waxes his car. "Especially if you're alone like I was."

"I know," I say, "that's what it's like for me down here too."

"Yeah," he says, a bit confused.

"Do you have any advice," I say, "about how to get through the early days? How to adjust faster?"

"Well . . . it helps if you find some common interests with people. Do you have any interests?"

Interests. Do I have any? Is "Tivo-ing" an interest? Probably not. At my old office, I once used rubber bands to construct a bouncing ball the size of a large mango. Does that count?

"I don't really have any," I say.

"Sure you do, kid, what kind of stuff do you like?" he says. "You collect something? Stamps?"

"Really, I don't have any interests," I say. "Nobody I know has any interests."

"Oh," he says. "That's too bad."

At that, the man goes back to waxing his car at six forty-five in the morning. I head back inside and go to sleep until noon.

MY ROOMMATES

MARGARET'S PARROT HAS TAUGHT ITSELF how to imitate my alarm clock. That becomes clear to me at five-thirty this morning, when three solid slaps delivered to my Sony Dream Machine fail to turn it off. The bird's alarm clock impression is impressive. A pitch-perfect crescendo of electronic beeps, rising in volume, piercing my sleep. BEEP! BEEP! BEEP! BEEP! BEEP! BEEP! BEEP! BEEP! BEEP! BEEP!

I get a kick out of it at first. I lie in bed and laugh. Then, after a while, it stops being funny. The parrot imitates my alarm clock every few minutes for two hours straight.

"I get it," I am forced to say, out loud, to a bird. "You can imitate the clock. Good one. You can stop now." But parrots don't have snooze bars. If you try to bop it on the head, you will just break its little bird neck.

When I moved in, I told my roommate, Margaret, I was okay with her cats and birds. Roommate Finders had told me I should be agreeable, so I lied and told her I was an animal enthusiast, and that I didn't mind if she moved the parrot onto the patio outside my bedroom.

"Outside, Zulu can get more fresh air," she said, and I said, "Great! Parrots need fresh air!"

What I probably should have said is: "Okay, but good luck finding fresh air if your cats keep taking dumps under my bed."

I lie down and try hard to fall asleep. I drift off and am sitting by the ocean, with the sun on my body and a line of turquoise hotels stretching horizon to horizon behind me. It's just like I had imagined Florida would be before I got here.

BEEP! BEEP! BEEP! BEEP! BEEP! BEEP! BEEP! BEEP! BEEP! BEEP!

My eyes snap open.

"Shut up, bird!" I shout, way too loudly.

There is a knock on my door, and it swings open before I say, "Come in." It is Margaret, her skinny body shrouded in a pale blue nightgown, coming back from her early-morning bathroom break. She glances over at the parrot to make sure I haven't killed it.

"Please!" she says to me.

She doesn't seem fazed by the fact that I am lying stark naked on top of the sheets. Margaret gives me a final reproachful glare and shuts the door. The parrot starts up again, BEEP! BEEP! BEEP! I hurl the throw pillow at the patio door. The bird keeps beeping.

Having a roommate can be practical, especially when you've just moved to a new place. I'm not yet sure, though, whether it is practical for me to have a roommate who spends the greater part of each afternoon talking to her animals. Ah, the Cat-and-Bird Lady. Back in suburbia, we would have dared each other to ring her doorbell and run. Now I live with her. Although it's not as if Margaret and I ever interact. Sometimes it seems like she's a ghost roommate, and that my real roommates are the cats, Ranchipurr and Petna, or the parrots, or the large painting of Jesus Christ that Margaret keeps on my bedroom wall.

Aren't Margaret and I a little too old to be platonic roommates? I haven't had a roommate in years. Once you get past a certain age, it's not considered appropriate. Which begs this additional question: Why would someone in her late sixties invite a twenty-eight-year-old man to live with her? Margaret never even asked me why I was down here in Florida. When I told her I was here to test out retirement early, she shrugged and went back to watching penguins on Animal Planet.

Is it financial problems? I've read that it's common for senior citizens to have inadequate savings. Does she like my company? Perhaps. It's not as if she has any friends stopping by. Maybe she likes the security of having a man around the house. Or maybe there's some darker reason. Margaret has a jittery way about her that can put me on edge. Her hair is often stringy and wild, as if she's been out wandering in the middle of the night. It's weird because she never leaves the condo. Sometimes, when I open the refrigerator and see the weird, drippy meat on Margaret's shelf, I wonder what it is I'm looking at. God help me. Is it an old cat? A former twenty-eight-year-old roommate? Later, at night, I stare from my bed at the painting of Jesus. I half expect eyes to blink behind the canvas, revealing the secret passage Margaret will use when she leaps into my room, in her pale blue nightgown, her wrinkled arms wielding a murderously sharp can opener.

In the living room, Margaret has a beautiful piano that she

never plays. Mainly the piano serves as a perch for Margaret's cats. The only time that Margaret talks to me is when I ask her about her cats.

"Ranchipurr is named after the Indian city Ranchipur," she tells me. "But I added an extra *r* because he's a cat, and cats purr."

"Oh," I say. I decide not to ask about Petna.

My friends in New York, Nick and Eva, have a pet cat. It's one of those things where the cat is an obvious surrogate for their future children, a bad omen considering that Nick tends to torment the cat with a laser pointer. Eva says that the reason Ranchipurr and Petna are always trying to run into my room is that it used to be their turf. She says that when someone new shows up in a cat's home, it's common for a turf war to break out.

"Oh, yes," my roommate Margaret told me once, "you're sleeping in Ranchipurr's and Petna's old playroom!" That would explain why there are cat hairs all over the carpet. Maybe it even explains the painting of Jesus. Maybe the cats are Catholic.

Ranchipurr is the more creepy-looking cat. He has a shock of gray-white hair sticking up from his forehead that makes him look like a deranged feline Don King. Petna is smaller and more cute; he's the "good cat" to Ranchipurr's "bad cat." Sometimes they'll both walk out onto the patio outside my bedroom, and there's nothing separating us but the glass sliding door. We've gotten into some lengthy staring contests like that on many afternoons. I always lose. I end up feeling vulnerable, and I go hide in the windowless bathroom for a while.

"I should have seen it coming," I tell Eva, "the moment I walked into Margaret's condo and smelled all that cat in the air. I just should have turned around and found another place to live."

"You're, like, obsessed with cats," she says.

"I spent three hours on the Internet last night reading about them. Is that obsessed?"

"Yes."

"Fact: they transport ear mites, germs, diseased fleas. Fact: in 2002, cats helped spread scrub typhus, a fatal disease, all over the Maldive Islands. And that's not the worst I've read about. Listen to this. Fact: a cat's litter box is filled with—"

"Rodney—"

"*Toxoplasma gondii,* a one-celled parasite that can do tremendous damage to an unborn baby. They recommend washing your hands after every single contact with a cat."

After a few more minutes, Eva tells me that I sound busy and that she will "let me go," and she goes back to work. I'm still wound up. Aren't cats supposed to play with yarn? These cats don't. Aren't they supposed to attack birds? I mean, these cats live with birds, and they don't attack them. I would feel better if the cats were attacking the birds. At least then my enemies would be going after one another, and I would benefit. But the cats and birds seem to have signed some historic cat-bird treaty where they agree to go after me instead.

The parrot begins squawking early every morning, and has a limited vocabulary. Sometimes it shouts "HEL-LOOOOOOO?!" imitating Margaret as she answers the phone. Other times, it repeats the only phrase that Margaret has taught it: "NOT TO WORRY! NOT TO WORRY! NOT TO WORRY! NOT TO WORRY! NOT TO WORRY! NOT TO WORRY!"

When a filthy bird shouts at me not to worry, I start to worry a lot more. It's not like I can tell the bird to shut the hell up. To begin with, Jesus is in my bedroom. I'm not Christian, but it's not like I want to curse in front of the dude. What if it turns out he's real? That's what I need, for the bird to imitate me saying "SHUT THE HELL UP," then Jesus gets pissed, and then Margaret kicks me out of the condo.

THE OL' SWIMMING HOLE

THERE ARE 108 condominium buildings in Century Village, clustered in groups around communal heated swimming pools. The swimming pool is the afternoon social center of our condominium cluster. Every day, after lunchtime, crowds of mainly female retirees gather there. From what I can tell, the mornings are full of activity for elderly retirees, and the afternoons are for sitting on your butt. Even though they're no longer working, they still seem to follow the same old rhythm of the workday, where nothing productive ever seems to happen between two and five.

Very few of the women go swimming. "I can't," I overhear one say. "I just went to the beauty parlor yesterday." That strikes me as funny. What's a little chlorine? As if her coiffure isn't chock-full of a billion chemicals already. Instead of swimming, the women pull the lounge chairs into circles and talk, all at once, for several hours. My grandmother used to do the same thing at her pool in Miami Beach, before she died, but I was always allowed to sit in with them because of the family connection. That's not the case here in Century Village.

I try to sit close enough to eavesdrop, to get a sense of the kinds of things I'll be talking about when I'm older. Mainly they gossip and talk about local restaurants or their failing health. Their conversations are like an avant-garde symphony of food and medical maladies; they often switch from one to the other and back again so fast I'm thoroughly confused.

"Have you been to Sweet Tomatoes yet?" I'll hear one say. "They got a lotta breads. I went there after Dr. Zann's."

"Dr. Zann, he's good," says another, resting her feet on a lounge chair. "Good man. I like the salads at Limburger's."

"I like that too. They make you wait too long, though."

"Yes, he's getting too popular. The other doctor at the clinic, he's not as good."

"I might go there tonight."

"Yeah?"

"Eat some greens. Make my doctor happy, right?"

When I get bored with eavesdropping on the women, I pretend to read a book until I fall asleep. I bought a copy of *The Old Man and the Sea* at a bookstore recently because it seemed both geographically and gerontologically appropriate. The book is something like twenty pages long and it's taken me almost a month to pretend to read it. It's getting to the point where I'm experiencing actual feelings of hate for the marlin on the book cover.

As difficult as it is to approach retirees when they're alone, it's way harder to do it when they're all together. They become an intimidating bloc. Their chairs are pressed together; they leave no room for anyone to come and join them. If I were to walk up to the Pool Group and start talking, I'd have to stand there like a dolt on the periphery of the circle. All those gray heads would turn at once, and I fear I would just be overwhelmed by my otherness and make an ass of myself. From what I've gathered I'm not overreacting.

"You don't barge in. People need to get used to you," a woman told me, speaking of her pool group, a few zones over. "It took me two years to get into the group."

Sometimes, if the Pool Group's conversation gets heated enough, I wake up. The mood becomes electric one afternoon when an ambulance drives into the parking lot and some emergency medical technicians get out and go into the building. It's a strange sight in the bright afternoon sun.

"Where are they going?" one of the women asks. They all begin to speculate on who has died or had a heart attack. We watch the elevator go up the building and stop on the third floor. The orderlies walk down the catwalk and stop at one of the condos.

"It's 303," says one of the women, an unnaturally redhaired woman named Shirley. "Is that the one from Philly? The short one?"

"No, she's in 308."

"Do we know 303?"

"Nope."

So the women turn away and continue their salad conversation.

Today they seem to be loudly complaining about Florida doctors who take Medicare subsidies and then charge patients more than they're supposed to. While I'm napping, a rotund woman I've never seen before lies down on the chaise next to me. She begins reading a Nora Roberts paperback while darting her eyes toward the Pool Group.

"Are you new?" I ask.

"Yes, I am," she says. "I moved here last week."

That's exciting to me. It's always easier to make friends with other new people, because you have at least one major thing in common.

"You're someone's grandson?" she says.

"Yes, I am," I say, which is really just a white lie. I am someone's grandson. They just happen to be over a thousand miles away right now.

"Are you making a lot of friends down here?" I ask her. Maybe she could introduce me to people.

"It's impossible to make friends here," she says. "Everyone is very cliquish." She motions to the group of women across from us, sitting in their circle of chairs. "Like them. That pow-wow there. They're a big clique."

"Oh," I say. "I'm sure they're very friendly." I've done some quick thinking and decided that I can perhaps send this woman over to the Pool Group as a weather balloon and see how they respond to an outsider.

"Them friendly?" she says. "I doubt it."

After fifteen minutes, the woman next to me stands up and walks over to the big clique. I can't believe it. She's going in.

"Excuse me," she says to the Pool Group. "I've been listening to your conversation about doctors who overcharge, and I just came over to say that all of you are wrong."

Now, personally, this wouldn't have been my opening statement if I were the weather balloon. It sounds a little confrontational to me. My weather balloon continues, telling the assembled women that she used to work for a doctor, and that he never overcharged patients who were on Medicare.

"Well, that's just one doctor up North," says Shirley, the fake redhead. "We're talking about a thousand doctors down here."

"You're all wrong," my weather balloon repeats, jabbing her finger at them.

"*You're* all wrong," Shirley repeats. "They charge more here. And it's against the law for them to do that. It's as against the law as if I were to punch you."

"Punch me?" says the weather balloon.

"I'm just using it as an example," says Shirley. The rest of the Pool Group begin to snicker.

"What a thing to say," says the weather balloon. She walks back over to me, deflated. I feel a brief sympathy for her. Man, the next twenty years of her life are going to be rough. Then I realize that the Pool Group might associate her with me, and I quickly face my body away from her so we look like strangers.

At four o'clock, like clockwork, everyone leaves to go get ready for dinner. Huge dark storm clouds are rolling in, like they do every late-summer afternoon in the Sunshine State. I go back to pretending to read my book.

Yeah, yeah, yeah, the old guy can't fish anymore. I get it.

In the late thirties and early forties, as Social Security took root, the state of Florida was beginning to enjoy unprecedented growth and development. By the end of World War II, it had emerged as a major vacation destination, which was a nice reversal of fortune for a once-beleaguered state. Before the twentieth century, Florida was the graveyard of countless Spanish explorers and their poor, loyal shipmen. It was blighted, mosquito-infested, chock-full of vindictive Seminoles; a swampy purgatory of real estate boondoggles. Sometimes it seemed like Spain and England were fighting over Florida to determine who had to keep it. It was the infected appendix of the American mainland.

But then, after World War II, the perfection of bug spray and affordable home air-conditioning made Florida a far more bearable place to be. Real estate developers began to sell the state as a vacation paradise, targeting GIs who had trained down in Florida and had fond memories of the state. In the first years after the war, Florida saw an increase in tourism many times over. And mind you, this was years before your children could be traumatized by a man in a mouse costume in broad Orlando daylight.

Soon, the real estate developers recognized that they were thinking too small. Why just sell Florida to vacationers? *People could live in Florida year-round!* The developers began one of the larger swamp-draining projects in the planet's history. They embarked on road shows up and down the East Coast, pitching their "retirement communities" as the perfect place to spend your golden years. They called these places Leisure City, Leisureville, Leisure Lakes, Leisure Village, and Serenity. Brochures promised year-round "resort living at its finest," a place "where living has no limits."

The pitch worked. The developers tapped in to an enormous population of spurned, dissatisfied elderly people with expendable incomes. These people had already been to Florida on vacation. They liked the idea of a holiday that would never end. Beginning in the 1950s, hundreds of thousands of recent retirees ventured south to Florida. They arrived in Florida at a rate of over one thousand people per week for almost thirty years, finally totaling over three million. It became a social necessity as much as a personal choice: If a retiree wanted to be with his lifelong friends from Brooklyn, he'd better move to Boca Raton. Soon mega-communities like Century Village appeared, reasonably priced and geared toward "active seniors." Century Village could house over eight thousand people in over a hundred condominium buildings. Within a few years it was virtually sold out.

Many of these communities prohibited any resident under the age of fifty-five. To me, that seems delightfully vengeful and vindictive. It's like an act of civil disobedience. Millions of senior citizens shouting, "You don't want us? We don't want you!" from the Florida peninsula, which suddenly resembled a giant downward-facing middle finger. It was a revolution, an octogenarian Boston Tea Party. The only difference was that these colonists would stick each tea bag in their purses for later use. Why let a perfectly good tea bag go to waste?

TERRY

THE POOL GROUP consists of about fifteen women and two men: Harvey and Al. Harvey and Al never say anything, though. They just sit there and let the women talk. The only time I hear them say anything is when they greet each other. "Hey fella!" they say. I love that. A lot of old men call one another "fella." It's what my grandfather calls me. I think it's an awesome term of endearment that deserves a comeback as soon as everyone gets tired of saying "dude" and "my nigga."

Harvey is round and Al is very skinny. They're a funny pair; they look like Mister Rogers crossed with Ernie and Bert. They're both widowers, and wear extremely yellow cardigan sweaters. It never seems to bother them when they show up in the same outfit. In general, I enjoy looking around the pool at everyone's retirement outfits. Most senior citizen retirees here spend their day in leisurewear: soft, loose, easy-to-wash cottons with bright, colorful, somewhat loony patterns. Elderly women often wear matching sets of clothing. They wear "outfits." Who does that other than babies and elderly women?

Shirley, the redhead from the Pool Group, explains it to me one day. "It's from back when we used to vacation," she tells me. "We used to dress up every day. Men would wear a shirt and tie every day. So our retirement clothes are different, they're crazy, they're wild! They let you know you're on permanent vacation!" One night, I see a ninety-year-old woman wearing a Hawaiian shirt, a white leather biker cap, and gigantic sunglasses.

The men wear unmatched clothes. It appears to be an act of defiance. They are outfit outlaws. At breakfast one day, I see a man whose every article of clothing is a different shade of blue. Light blue slacks, dark blue cardigan sweater, royal blue baseball hat, blue socks, and navy striped sneakers. He looks like Mister Rogers crossed with Cookie Monster. I doubt he spent more than a few seconds pulling those clothes together; no fretting in front of the mirror worrying about whether his light blue slacks went with his dark blue shoes.

Elderly retirees class it up when they're going out for the night. The women wear blouses, sweater sets, brooches, and makeup. There is a weakness for enormous earrings. The men often wear blazers, especially if they're going dancing afterward. On the plane down to Florida, I sat next to a man wearing a blazer. He looked at my T-shirt. It had a cartoon dragon eating ice cream on it.

"Is that how you travel?" he asked.

One afternoon, on a whim, I purchase a zip-up white terrycloth shirt in a local flea market. Back home, if I wore a terrycloth shirt, it would be tantamount to personally inviting people to kick my ass. I wear my shirt to the pool one afternoon. What fabric is better than terry cloth? It is extremely comfortable. I feel like I am wearing a koala bear. The late-afternoon sun is shining down on me. A breeze blows into the terry cloth and through my chest hair, cooling me off. I know I look good. Several hours pass, and the sun begins to dip low in the sky. My cell phone vibrates in the pocket of my cargo shorts, and rather than answer it, I just let it massage my lower thigh. After a long while, I open my eyes, and Harvey and Al are crossing past me in their matching yellow cardigans, lit from behind by a halo of warm orange.

"How you doing?" I say.

"Hey fella," says Al.

All around, I have to admit that felt pretty good.

TWILIGHT

At five most evenings I hop in my rental car and go out for dinner. It's comforting but weird to drive the same Florida roads that we used to drive in the rental convertible when I was a kid, visiting my grandparents. Back then the Lionel never stopped oozing from the radio. Will there even be convertibles when I retire again, later in life? Will there be Lionel?

This retirement, I rented the cheapest car possible, a Spectra. It's a flimsy automobile with the acceleration of a sea monkey. I like that it forces me to drive with caution, like an older person might. Whenever I pull out into the street from Century Village, the other cars get backed up behind me, waiting for my car's pickup to kick in. They're young professionals who just finished work and can't bear to wait. They end up honking and speeding past me on the road's apron. I know it's old people that have the bad driving reputations, but I can tell you firsthand that it's thirty-five-year-olds who drive like assholes.

I'm amazed by how many retirees eat all their meals out. Nobody cooks anymore. The only people I've met who claim they cook are a few widower men who dutifully try to follow their late wives' yellowed recipes. It's a way for old men to pick up old women, because the women, at least the women I've spoken to, do not cook. I'm learning that the whole "just like Grandma used to make" saying is bogus.

"I cooked for forty years," a woman in the clubhouse said to me the other day. "Why would I want to cook now? Let somebody else cook for a change."

Value is the big concern for people who are living and eating on fixed incomes. At local supermarkets, there is a senior citizen traffic jam at the free sample areas. I've never seen a person work harder than the man dispensing these samples—his bicep is thick from handling thousands of pita crisps an hour. "Go check out The Boys," one woman told me, recommending one of the local markets. "You can eat a whole meal there for free!" But for senior citizens, the quest for value doesn't end at scamming free meals at the supermarket. The seniors at Century Village also flock to the many local restaurants that offer complete meals for under ten dollars, as long as you show up to eat before 6 P.M. These are, of course, known as "early bird" or "twilight" specials.

For a young man, it feels very unnatural to be eating dinner at a quarter to five. It's summertime, and the light outside is still bright. My body seems to be saying to me: "Are you for real, dude?" I have to force myself. I've been going to all the senior citizen standbys: Bagels by Star, the Bountiful Buffet, the Two Jay's Deli, and, of course, Nestor's, one of the most famous early bird restaurants in South Florida.

At Nestor's, you get soup, an entrée, a beverage, dessert, and a complimentary offering of coleslaw and challah bread. And, if you arrive between 3 and 5 P.M., your bill comes to less than nine dollars. Thriftiness! I always challenge myself to order the thing on the menu that seems the most "senior citizen–y." I try to make a game out of it; what food sounds most like old-person food? Breakfast is easy. I just go to Bagels by Star, and for $1.99 I get oatmeal, which seems like the perfect old-person breakfast; oatmeal is what happens to bacon and eggs after they retire. As far as dinner, the gold-medal-winning dish so far is baked scrod. I've been eating that several times a week. I suppose that part of me believes that if I eat like my fellow retirees do, it will give me some kind of edge as far as gaining their trust. They will smell the scrod on my breath, or the matzo-ball molecules I am sweating out, and stop viewing me as an interloper.

The prepared fish notwithstanding, eating healthy at an early bird restaurant isn't easy. Nutrition is often pitted against a good bargain, and the bargain wins out. One local health club employee phrased it to me this way: "These older people, they get dessert, cheesecake, free with dinner. I tell them not to eat dessert; they always say, 'But it comes with it!' That's the thinking. How can you cut something bad out if it comes for free?" But she also adds that this quality is more characteristic of older senior citizens—the ones that grew up during the Great Depression.

"The baby boomers, the health nuts, they're a whole other thing. But we'll see if they can keep that low-carb diet up once they have someone waving free cheesecake in their face."

At 5:45 most evenings, I'm done eating dinner. It feels weird, because at that time of the day I tend to be finishing a late lunch. But overpowering the weirdness is a strong and unexpected sense of accomplishment. When you finish eating dinner before six, you have the entire rest of the evening to do whatever you want with. It's a pretty good feeling. I'm starting to think elderly people might be on to something.

But I only manage to eat early a few nights a week. I keep messing up. Some nights I'll find myself hunched over in my car eating McDonald's cheeseburgers at 10 P.M. What retiree would do that? Other nights I will be sucked toward some neon Jimmy Buffett–themed restaurant, and before I can stop myself I have had an onion haystack, mozz sticks, and three tall glasses of some concoction called "the Swiss Monkey."

One Friday evening I experience total meltdown. Instead of going to Nestor's for scrod, I go to a sushi restaurant and eat sushi. I don't show up until eight-thirty. I feel as if I've committed some kind of mortal retiree sin. Not just because of the late hour but because very few people over the age of seventy eat sushi. The worst of it is, the sushi in South Florida is not even good. It's horrible, rubbery, unsatisfying sushi. It tastes kind of like scrod. It's weird: you'd think that a state surrounded by water on three sides could get it together on the sushi.

I drive back to Margaret's in a gloomy mood. The moon is illuminating a sky full of strange, billowing Florida thunderclouds. Once again, it's going to rain in the Sunshine State. I've never seen skies like I've seen in summertime Florida. Apocalyptic. This whole retirement experiment is starting to take on a doomed feel. Florida is so much darker and more foreign than I remember it as a kid. The state just feels unlucky. My crackpot late-night theory: There are too many elderly people down here, maybe, and they don't need luck anymore, just time, so luck has moved on. Maybe that's why all that weird stuff is always happening here, the hurricanes, the shark attacks, the hanging chads, voting Republican in 2004, and those doctors who amputated the wrong leg.

As I drive home, I'm thinking about Margaret's big, shiny, never-used piano. What a lonely piano! I decide to call someone up North to chat. Everyone is out for Friday night. Usually I have no problem getting my friends on the phone, because they're at work and locked down at their desks. I go through my cell phone directory. Alex, Ali, Amanda, Amy—Where is everyone? Am I missing something amazing? Then I remind myself that when I was up North, in my real life, Friday nights were never that much fun anyway. All that pressure to be out partying. Have I ever actually succeeded at partying, even for a second?

I call my grandmother in New Jersey instead. Maybe she and my grandfather will be watching *JAG* or something, and it will help me feel less lame by comparison. It turns out that she is in bed reading while Grandpa e-mails. Good enough.

"You're just finishing eating now?" my grandmother says, after she picks up the phone. "It's so late! It's almost ten!"

She asks me if I'm looking forward to my twin sister's wedding. Will I be bringing a date? It would be great to see me settled down with someone. I get off the phone. I don't feel like going home and dealing with Margaret and our condo, so I drive to the nearest multiplex and spend an hour ogling local seventeen-year-olds in spaghetti-strap tank tops. Somehow that makes me feel a little better. I might not be able to eat like my grandmother does, but at least I'm having no problem being a dirty old man.

After midnight, Century Village is quiet and dark, save for an ambulance making its way through the community to destination unknown. Its lights are flashing, but it is making no noise so as not to wake anyone. I consider following it out of curiosity—maybe it's someone I know—but decide to drive home instead. I enter Margaret's darkened condo and brace myself for the hot gust of cat. But Margaret has gone to sleep, and mercifully, so have the animals.

I lie in bed for a moment, staring at the Jesus painting next to my bed. He's knocking meekly on a door in some far-off casbah. A question pierces my mind: Can I masturbate in front of Jesus? Can I? Spaghetti-strap tank tops! Back tattoos! But I can't. I'm not Christian, but I can't. The same old bedroom logic. What if it turns out that Christians are right about everything, and Jesus rises again? O Jesus, kind Jesus, knocking meekly on a door. I bet he would be especially pissed at me in this case. He would not knock on my door; he would kick it in for sure, or better yet, blow it to bits with a wave of his hand. So I just turn over, close my eyes, and go to sleep sushi-side down.

"Is it because he's Jesus?" my friend Jenni will later say over the phone, "or just because there's another guy in the room?"

JOINERS

THERE ARE WELL OVER ONE HUNDRED CLUBS at Century Village. There's a fishing club, canasta club, shuffleboard club, tennis club, table tennis club, bridge club, duplicate bridge club. There are social clubs for Brooklynites, Staten Islanders, New Jerseyans, Canadians, computer users, Democrats and Republicans (inactive for years), and Jewish war vets. There's an art appreciation club, a Japanese bunka club, and a line dance club.

The woman in the Activities Office recommends the Newcomers Club to me. It's a club for new members of the community to get together and enjoy some entertainment. She still goes to it, even though she has been at Century Village for years.

"Is it a good place to get to know people?" I ask.

"They serve snacks," she says. "That's why you go to these things."

I've been reading a lot of lengthy books on aging lately. It's good swimming pool reading, much better than Hemingway. *Successful Aging* is a good one. It was written based on the findings of the MacArthur Study, a decadelong study by PhDs in a variety of disciplines on the qualities that separate "successful agers" from bad agers. One distinction it draws is that "successful agers" tend to stay actively involved in the activities and events of the retirement community. They stay physically, mentally, and socially engaged. The MacArthur Study showed that these people live longer, healthier lives. Bad agers are more likely to stick to themselves and fall into a rut. They suffer more chronic illnesses and diseases, and tend to die earlier. I've seen all kinds here at Century Village. The women at the swimming pool seem like successful agers. I suspect my roommate Margaret might be a bad ager. What's scary to me is that sometimes I relate more to Margaret. Is that why Roommate Finders put us together? Did they look at us and say, "Hey, let's let these two fruitcakes go down together."?

Joining clubs can be important for the overall well-being of older people. "With lack of stimulation comes a subtle but serious reduction in mental functioning," says *Successful Aging*. I don't think that bodes well for people my age. My generation might be bad agers in training. Most people that I know regard joining clubs as passé and campy. They think joining is for Scientologists; they'll maybe join a gym, or Netflix, but that's it.

My Newcomers Club table has eight elderly retirees sitting around it. A straw poll when I first arrive reveals that I am the only actual newcomer here. There are maybe fifty retirees here in all. It's early afternoon, and everyone is a little sluggish and perhaps would rather be at the pool. The president of the Newcomers Club gives a brief speech before we begin. She lays out the agenda. Later on, we will be enjoying a singer named Carl, who she promises us has a "liquid chocolate" voice. But the first half hour will be taken up by a representative from a financial company, who will be giving a presentation on the benefits of Medicare-friendly annuities. That's typical, I've learned; club meetings are increasingly sponsored by companies who pay for the snacks and entertainment. That way, retirees don't have to lay out any of their money to fund the club. In return, they have to listen to a lengthy presentation intended to separate them from their money.

"Okay, people!" says the company representative. You can tell she does this a thousand times a week. She gazes around the room and then begins to shout at the top of her lungs. "Okay! We know what you're afraid of! Your husband gets sick! You're worried you might have a health crisis and get put on assisted living and go through all your money! But there's something you can do! We're experts in it!"

Nobody at my table seems to be paying any attention whatsoever. We're like bored ten-year-olds suffering through a safety demonstration, but this one doesn't end with the titillation of watching a grown man in a police uniform making out with a mannequin. What's worse is that because this woman won't be quiet, the whole point of the club is lost. Nobody gets to talk to anybody.

"Remember," the representative shouts, "there are no problems! Only solutions!"

We clap politely. Then the singer comes out. He is a young, energetic man singing standards along with a RadioShack karaoke machine. His voice, I notice, is not liquid chocolate. It's far too overwrought, more like a candy bar left too long on the dashboard. It isn't until the end of the meeting that anything special happens. The president stands back up. "Well," she says, "this wouldn't be the Newcomers Club if we didn't meet some newcomers. So, everybody! Turn to the person to your right and introduce yourself!" I look to my right. There's a dangerously skinny man there whom I haven't talked to for the entire meeting.

"Hi, I'm Rodney," I say.

"Hi, Rodney. I'm Glen."

"Okay," says the leader. "Now hug the person to your right."

Glen and I stare at each other for an awkward few seconds. Other than my grandparents, I don't think I've ever hugged an old person before. But I give it a shot. I lean in, taking care not to snap his spine in two. I hear myself saying, "Heyyyy!," which somehow makes me feel more comfortable. His body is tiny and smells like cologne. It feels like I'm hugging a peppermint stick.

Though I have a functional car, when I have to get around Century Village I take the bus. Many in the community take the bus because they have given up their automobiles. Often, a worried son up North forces his parent to stop driving after the first minor fender bender. It's a sad rite of passage, loss of independence and all that.

The bus stops at every single one of the Century Village zones, and then stops at the clubhouse. Other buses take you to nearby shopping centers and back. It would take me less time to walk to these places, but I like the public transportation. It's good people-watching time, and you can strike up the occasional conversation with a seatmate, or you can eavesdrop. I recognize Shirley the redhead from the Pool Group in my zone. It's impossible to approach her at the pool, but on the bus, it's more manageable. The slow-moving deer has been separated from the herd.

"Hey," I say to her, "don't you live in Exeter?" I'm referring to the "condominium association" we live in, one of sixteen in Century Village.

"Yes, I do," she says. "I've seen you at the pool, haven't I? You're the young man who lives with that odd woman on the ground floor?"

Shirley introduces herself. We begin to talk. She's in her early seventies. Her red hair is cut in a stylish bob and her outfit displays more subtlety and discretion than the typical garish Pool Group ensembles.

"I have friends all over Century Village," says Shirley. "Here on the bus, I have bus friends. At the pool, I have pool friends. They're different from my bus friends. Then I have canasta friends; they're different too."

"I want to play canasta!" I say, a little too enthusiastically. A lot of people around the community play canasta. I thought it might be worth learning while I was down here, to get a sense of what retirees do. But it's harder than you'd think to get invited.

"I'll teach you," Shirley says. "You can come to my game." She doesn't offer any additional information, though, like where or when her game is played.

When my bus stop comes up, it's Shirley's stop too. I wait a minute for her to get off the bus before I do, so we don't have to awkwardly continue our conversation while filing out. But she waits for me outside and gives me a quick hug good-bye, and I think: Gosh, I'm hugging a lot of old people lately.

At the swimming pool one afternoon, Shirley invites me to come over and sit down with the Pool Group.

"What are you doing over there?" she shouts. "Come here!" She introduces me to the rest of the group. "I met him on the bus!" she says.

"I'm her bus friend," I say, making it seem like a joke, in case she disagrees.

"Yes," she says, "he's my bus friend! He's my strapping-young-man bus friend!" She turns to the rest of the club. "He wants to play canasta," she says. They all laugh like that's a hilarious joke.

It must make a big difference that Shirley has acknowledged me in public, because a miracle then occurs. The Pool Group makes some space for me and allows me to pull up a chaise. I sit there, in the Pool Group. I keep waiting for them to kick me out, but it doesn't happen. Across the pool, I see my deflated weather balloon giving me a look that says "hey, sellout" from behind her sunglasses. I end up sitting next to Al, one of the yellow-cardigan twins.

"How ya doing, fella?" he says, real cool.

"I saw you in the clubhouse the other day," says a small woman in a wheelchair. "At the Newcawmahs Club, and then at the Not Faw Women Only Club."

Ah, the old-school Brooklyn accent. There are no *r*'s in South Florida.

"Y'aw very active," says another woman, sounding impressed.

"He's a young man," says Al, glancing at me on my chaise lounge, "of course he's active."

It feels great to be sitting in the Pool Group. I was beginning to think it would never happen. I thought it was impossible for me to fit in. Things operate on a different schedule down here, I guess. Immediate gratification takes almost a month.

KAWAMOTA

THE POOL GROUP is preoccupied with the fact that I am living with Margaret. Led by Shirley and Paula, they pepper me with questions for hours. There's a cliché I've heard, that elderly people are set in their ways and threatened by change or anything different. I don't know if that's true yet, but I know this: Margaret is asocial and unusual, and the Pool Group finds that unnerving.

Paula in particular is always probing me for dirt about Margaret. Paula is without a doubt the worst of the Pool Group gossips, so I always tread carefully. She lives directly above Margaret and me. Once she invited me up to her condo, and I was overwhelmed by how nice it was compared with ours. The same layout, but way cleaner and nicer, with shiny white tile floors and far less parrot and Jesus. The condo felt like the least haunted place I have ever been, which is funny, since our whole building is probably built on an Indian burial ground.

"So . . . you live with Margaret!" Paula says to me one day by the pool.

"Yes," I say.

"I once tried to say hello to her. She scurried inside like I yelled 'Boo!' "

"Well, she's shy," I say. That's a ridiculous understatement. Margaret hardly ever talks to me, and I *live* with her. It's even quieter in our condo than in that room I had early on at college, when I lived with the weird French guy who made his bed every fifteen minutes.

"Doesn't she have pets?" says Shirley.

"No," I say, "she doesn't have pets."

Margaret, in one of the few times she ever spoke to me, made me promise never to tell anyone that she keeps pets. It's strictly against Century Village rules. The reason is simple: there's a prevailing attitude among most retirement community administrators that elderly people will not be able to take proper care of their animals. If a dog misses a few feedings and accidentally gets let out, then you've got a problem. You've got an innocent eighty-year-old with teeth marks on her ankle and a massive lawsuit on your hands.

"She does too have pets," says Paula.

"No, she doesn't."

"Yes, she does," says Paula. "I know she does. My husband says he's heard birds down there. And I've seen that cat staring out the window at me with that little black face."

"Cats?" I say. "I've never seen cats in there."

"I didn't say *cats*," says Paula, gloating. "I said *cat*."

"That's what I said. I've never seen a cat in there."

That's what I am trying to convince Paula of. That I have "never seen a cat in there." That I have somehow failed to notice the two animals that keep sneaking into my bedroom and taking secret shits under my bed.

"I know she has pets," says Paula. "You can say whatever you want. I know. Everyone knows."

I think all my phone calls home are starting to irritate my friends.

"I hate the fact that, whenever you want, you can make a loud bell ring in my office," Nick said to me the other day. "Have you heard of e-mail?"

I call my friends and family way more than I did before I moved to Florida. I keep telling them it's part of the adjustment process. It's jarring to move to a strange place and live with a strange person. My friend Jill told me the other day that she doesn't buy it. She thinks the problem is that my life down here in the retirement community lacks structure.

"This retirement thing has made you soft," Jill suggests. "You're incapable of solving, like, the simplest problems. If the condo is so weird, why don't you move out or make it better?"

I disagree with her on the softness issue. I don't think retirement has made me soft. In fact, I think it was working that made me soft. It's not like I did all that much when I had a seventy-hour-a-week job. I was "at work." I wasn't working. If anything, I was just making compulsive lists of things that I needed to do so that I would run out of time to do them. I'm still confused about that: How can you be overworked and underemployed at the same time?

So I decide to make a list.

Things I Can Do to Make the Condo More Livable

1) Replace the old bedsheets Margaret gave me with new ones.

2) New pillow that doesn't have mystery stain on it.
3) Deodorize anything cat may have touched.
4) Unpack my bags.
5) Talk to Margaret more.

The first four tasks are easy. A trip to Target and a few hours of unpacking rejuvenate my bedroom. Target sells tapestries, and I consider purchasing one and covering up the Jesus painting with it. That would solve the whole problem. I could even patent it and market it to men in a similar situation. I could call it a "Jesus Sheath," or maybe a "Shroud of Boca."

Task Five: One early morning Margaret comes to the breakfast table wearing a lovely dress and makeup. It's the first time I've seen her in anything other than her nightgown. Her wiry brown hair has been drawn into a neat bun.

"Wow!" I say. "You're all dressed up! Going anywhere special?"

"To the doctor's," she says.

"Gosh. Is everything okay?"

"Yeah . . . it's just a follow-up appointment. . . ."

"Going kind of early, huh?" I say. It's about six forty-five.

"Well," she says, "I need to take three buses to get there."

"I have a car," I tell her. "I could give you a ride if you want."

"Yeah?" she says. "It wouldn't be any trouble?"

"No no no no no no," I say. Definitely saying no a few times too many to appear sincere. "No trouble at all. Most exciting thing I'll do all day, probably."

"Okay," she says. "If it's no trouble."

It seems like Margaret has never been in a car before. She rides in the passenger seat, sitting straight forward in a rigid, unnatural way. It creates a rotten center of gravity, and it seems every time I turn the wheel Margaret slides across the seat. It's as if I'm chauffering a terrified cat.

"What did you used to do for a living before you were retired?" I ask Margaret.

"I was a piano teacher," she says.

"Piano teacher?"

"Yes."

"I never hear you play the piano," I say.

"I don't play anymore," she says. "Not very often."

Piano teacher! I want to burst out laughing. When I was young, I used to take violin lessons from Ms. Kawamota. It was torture. Every Tuesday evening my parents would drop me off, and I would be trapped in a house with the woman, her metronome, her phony plastic fruit, until my parents came to pick me up. It all makes perfect sense now. For the last four weeks, I've been living with Ms. Kawamota. I've been at the longest music lesson of my life. Perhaps that's why I've been calling people up North all the time. Because I've been at Ms. Kawamota's for a month, and nobody is coming to pick me up.

We drive down Boynton Beach Boulevard toward the doctor's. Early-morning traffic is picking up, the sun is rising now. I catch a glint of light off Margaret's finger.

"Are you married?" I ask. I'm trying to make her feel more at ease.

"Yes," Margaret says. "He passed away two years ago."

"I'm sorry."

"Yes. He was a piano teacher too."

"It must be hard for you with him gone," I say.

"He's not gone," Margaret snaps. "He still watches over me. He's in the condo all the time. I don't know what I would do if he was gone."

"Right," I say. "Absolutely."

"Are you married?" she says.

"No," I say. "But my twin sister is going to get married next month."

"How old are you?" she says.

"I'm twenty-eight."

I fiddle with the air conditioner for a few minutes, so Margaret is comfortable.

"So are you going to the doctor for a checkup?" I ask.

"I'm on psychotropic medication," she says. "To deal with my feelings of loss." She says it like she's reading it out of a book.

"Wow," I say. "Yeah. I bet. I can only imagine." Then I say nothing for a while. We take a hard left turn and Margaret slides across the seat.

"I ran out of pills a few weeks ago," she says. "I stay in bed more when that happens."

"Oh," I say. "Yeah, you should get some more pills, definitely."

We get to the doctor's office. I watch Margaret walk into the large chrome building and disappear. I wait for half an hour for her to come out. I have an urge to take my phone out and call a friend, but I fight it off.

Part Two

SARASOTA SOFTBALL

> There is a simple, basic fact about exercise and your health: fitness cuts your risk of dying. It doesn't get much more "bottom line" than that.
>
> —*Successful Aging*

"I'M VERY ATHLETIC," Stuart tells me, as we drive to his Senior League softball game. I doubt this, and the reason is simple: he is wearing jean shorts. How athletic can someone be if he wears jean shorts to play a competitive sport? Perhaps it's unfair to hold a seventy-year-old man up to my high standards in sports fashion. While Stuart starts to brief me on the opposing team, I zone out, thinking: How are ordinary jeans so right and jean shorts so wrong? Somewhere in those extra two feet of fabric lies the difference between being a sex symbol and a camp counselor.

I was introduced to Stuart by a young acquaintance of mine back home. The first time I spoke to him, he invited me over to the Gulf coast of Florida to watch him play a scrimmage game in the Senior Softball League of Sarasota. He plays three times a week.

"I saw an ad in the paper looking for seniors interested in playing softball," he tells me. "I really missed playing ball, so I figured I'd give it a shot. You're pretty good at sports, right?"

"Yeah," I say. "I used to be really good. Back when I used to play them, when I was a kid."

"I can tell," Stuart says, looking me over. "You have an athlete's build."

Stuart himself is in his late sixties, about five-seven, with a compact body and a gap in his teeth large enough to drive a base hit through. His skin is pale from sitting indoors writing mystery novels. He's won an Edgar Award for his work. One of his more popular creations is Abe Lieberman, a small-framed crime-fighting Jew working the city streets of Chicago, where Stuart grew up. "I used to love playing ball when I was a kid," Stuart says, turning left into a large park. "We'd play Windy City ball. Every time I go out there it's like I'm reliving my childhood."

"Yeah," I say, still ruminating about jean shorts. "Childhood was awesome."

"Most of the guys in the league are in their seventies," says Stuart. "We have some players in their eighties too. We even have one who's eighty-seven. He's a Mennonite. He plays second base." I tell Stuart that I'm not sure what a Mennonite is.

"It's very similar to the Amish," he tells me.

"Amish people are allowed to play softball?"

"I suppose so. Eli does."

"Is he good?"

"Oh, he's phenomenal," Stuart says. "Very fast."

Years of watching the last five minutes of local news broadcasts gives you a precise expectation of what a Senior League softball team would look like: round-backed, ravaged old men wearing promotional baseball caps their children sent to them from the company picnic. Lots of high-fiving at home plate to the tune of ragtime music.

These are not those men. These old men are scary.

That's my first thought upon viewing the players in the softball league. They are enormous. They are strapping. A few players are fat, but fat in a sturdy, John Madden way rather than a John Candy way. I had just read about sarcopenia, in *Successful Aging,* which it defined as the normal deterioration of muscle mass that occurs in old age. Maybe somebody forgot to tell these guys about sarcopenia.

Alan is the first to approach us. He is easily 250 pounds, the kind of guy who would be nicknamed "Bear" or "Buddy." Another guy, 275 pounds at least, actually *is* nicknamed Buddy. Buddy used to be a referee for the World Wrestling Federation. I make the mistake of asking Buddy whether professional wrestling is rigged. "Look at my medical bills from those years," he says. "Tell me if those are rigged."

They amble onto the field, and I watch them go. "They're huge," I say. "Yeah," says Stuart, nearby, with a mixture of pride and fear. "They're big Midwestern boys. They can play ball too."

To generalize, the Atlantic coast of Florida, where I live, is composed of predominantly Jewish retirees from the Northeast. The Gulf coast of Florida is brimming with retirees from the Midwest. The reason for this, many people agree, is surprisingly simple. I-75, the main north–south interstate of the Midwest, dumps you off on the Gulf coast. I-95 dumps you off on the Atlantic coast. Once again, good old American laziness wins the day. This migration pattern has resulted in a wide gulf between the two Florida coasts in such areas as softball-playing ability, bagel type identification proficiency, ability to hold hard liquor, and Mennonite foot speed.

Atlantic coast residents don't always seem like born athletes. A lot of them picked up sports recently, at the request of their doctors. But the Gulf coasters here at the baseball diamond seem like born athletes. Many of them played baseball in college or semiprofessionally. One after another, the men take practice swings, and you can see in their effortless ease the countless thousands of pop flies they hit to their teammates, their buddies, their children, and their grandchildren. Even Eli the Mennonite, a tiny man with a massive white Amish beard, looks slick and experienced, fielding ground balls so stylishly I expect him to get called up to the show any minute. I bet when he was a kid he made his own baseballs, from twine, rye, maybe sun-hardened pig fat.

One of the more perfect-looking players, Bob Hover, steps up next to me, tossing a baseball up and down. "So Stuart tells me you're a writer," he says. I tell him I am. It turns out Bob is a retired soap opera actor who used to play a doctor on *Another World*. "I once read one of Stuart's books," he says, "the one with the rabbi detective?" "He's not a rabbi," I say, "he's just Jewish." Bob shrugs and turns to the field. "Pretty sad, huh? Bunch of old guys playing softball." "No," I say, maybe with some condescension, "it's inspiring that you guys are still out there giving it a go." "Yeah, right." He laughs, bouncing the baseball off the inside of his tanned elbow, then flashing a perfectly white TV-doctor smile.

I stand on the field, feeling disassociated and strange. It is not nostalgia—fresh-cut grass, the sweet aroma of linseed oil, and all that Bob Costas erotica. No, the sensation I'm experiencing is a kind of mortal fear—the fear of organized sports. Because let's be honest at this point—I was not a good athlete, ever. I still can't throw a spiral. I was asked on several occasions by my lacrosse team to get out of uniform and serve as timekeeper. And as for baseball, the sport where you are most on your own, most dependent on your own ability, I remember nothing but pure misery. The misery of standing in left field, baseball Siberia, praying that one of my fellow ten-year-olds wouldn't somehow hit puberty mid at-bat and find the strength to hit one at me. The misery of eking out a base hit with your eyes squeezed shut, followed by the paralyzing awareness that you might be expected to run the bases.

The men split into two evenly matched teams and the game begins. The rhythm of the senior softball game is unlike that of any softball game I've ever witnessed. The defining factor is that most of the men have much stronger arms and shoulders than legs. For all of them, the knees have started to go. "It's what you get for carrying this kinda weight around for so long," Buddy, the WWF referee, says to me, slapping his ample belly for emphasis. Because of this, senior softball is very much a hitter's game—as long as the hitters can get the ball in play and keep it low, odds are the fielders won't be able to reach it in time.

The opposite side of the "strong arms/weak legs" issue is this—the hitters, once they put a ball in play, run very slowly. And the fielders, once they reach the ball, have the arm strength to fire the ball wherever it needs to go. So when people do get out, it's in ways I have never seen before—like someone hitting a line drive deep into the hole in left center, and then getting thrown out at first.

So far, this physical lopsidedness is working in favor of Stuart's team. They've already scored three runs and put several runners on base by the time Stuart goes up to bat. Next to these silver-haired Goliaths, Stuart looks tiny, like one of the Japanese boys who used to play on my Little League team—except Stuart doesn't have a bowl haircut or weird-looking Velcro sneakers.

Stuart assumes a gawky batting stance and waits for his pitch. I watch, a pit of nervousness expanding wider and wider in my stomach. I would really like to see Stuart get on base. It's a natural pheromonal instinct that I have to root for the smallest Jewish guy on a playing field. Call it spaz solidarity. When there is no Jewish guy on the playing field, which is often, you root for the guy with the most Jewish name, like Troy Aikman or Ryne Sandberg.

The first pitch comes in and Stuart manages to miss it by several inches. The pitcher tosses another one, and the pitch is way inside, brushing Stuart back. I find myself reminiscing about a big baseball discovery I made when I was about eleven. After several years of limited success getting on base, I found that the odds improved if I stood a lot closer to the plate. It didn't improve my hitting at all, but it did significantly increase my chances of getting hit by a pitch. For that one glorious year, before anyone was capable of pitching the ball particularly hard, I got on base all the time. I'd even lower a shoulder on purpose into the ball path, knowing that the brief sting of pain would soon be superceded by a sense of relief and achievement when I got to take my base. The baseball fathers took to facetiously calling me "Iron Man," but, as I couldn't yet recognize facetiousness, I took it as a great compliment.

I consider calling a conference with Stuart and passing my wisdom on, but it's too late. A pitch comes in, and Stuart swings and makes contact. The ball arches up, a classic pop fly. Stuart ignores the ball's inevitable fate and runs to first as fast as he can, his palms facing the ground as if he's running on tacks. The second baseman catches it without much of a problem. Stuart returns to the bench. "Good contact," his teammates say, and Stuart beams.

Ah, yes. "Good contact." That brings back memories.

Turning my attention back to the game, I see that a player with a strong physical resemblance to the author Tom Wolfe is now at the plate. It occurs to me that you're not a legitimate sports fan when the first thing you think when you see a guy hitting is "Hey, he looks like New Journalist Tom Wolfe without the white suit." Tom Wolfe is running the count up high, and when he gets the pitch he's been waiting for, he swings, gorgeously. The ball sails toward center field, where TV Dr. Bob is already backpedaling, tracking the ball's path with surgical precision. Bob leaps and somehow comes down with the ball. It's incredible. All the old-timers on our bench jump carefully to their feet and erupt in a spontaneous cheer, forgetting for a moment which team they're on. None of us notices Tom Wolfe returning to the dugout, clutching his back, and grimacing. "I strained it," he says, and he starts to pack his duffel bag. I half expect TV Dr. Bob to run in and confirm the diagnosis, but he just looks on with an expression of studied concern.

Typically, this is when your high school coach would start barking, "Suck it up!," but that's not how old men play sports. Whatever there is to gain from pain, they've gained enough of it by the time they're sixty-five. "So long," says a guy on the bench. "Go home to your loving wife." "Yeah," says another guy, "we hear your wife is very loving." "I think you mean his husband," says another guy. Everyone laughs really hard, and it seems to restore our collective machismo—you can give a man a bad back, but you can never take away his inalienable right to imply another man is a cuckold or a homo.

The other team has come in from the field, and Stuart points out that his team is now one short. "So play one short; you're already kicking our ass," says the opposing team's pitcher. "How about the kid? Can he play?"

All eyes turn to me, and I start waving my hands and shaking my head. "No, that's okay. I'm really here to watch." They stare back at me, and I sense I haven't quite made a compelling argument yet. "I don't even have a glove," I add, knowing as soon as I've said it that it is a tactical error.

"Here, use mine. I don't need it while we're batting," says TV Dr. Bob, and he tosses his glove at me.

When I come to my senses I'm standing somewhere in the

outfield next to Stuart. I think I instinctively ran for the outfield, because it is the farthest you can get from the ball. Stuart takes advantage of another Jew on the field to climb up one rung on the outfield ladder. "Why don't you play left field," Stuart says to me, "and I'll switch to center left."

So I am home again, in the queasy black void of left field. Yet, nobody knows I belong in left field. I have a fresh start. If I can survive out here and not screw up, they'll just assume I know what I'm doing. Not only that, but maybe, in the fifteen-year downtime since my last baseball game, I have somehow transformed into a gifted baseball player. After all, I'm much taller and much stronger. I've done probably several thousand sit-ups since I was twelve years old. Maybe my body will just know how to get the job done now. I need only sit back and watch, like I watch a baseball game on TV.

Alan, playing first base, takes a few steps into left field and asks me, "Hey, kid, you want a warm-up throw?" I say, "Nah, I'm good," but Alan throws one anyway. It's a soft throw, and I catch it without much of a problem. I wind up and throw the ball back to Alan. Not wanting my ball to fall short of him, I overcompensate. My throw, following a sickly, lopsided trajectory, ends up thirty feet beyond him. It rolls past our Mennonite second baseman and to the feet of Doug, our massive shortstop.

They look at the ball, and then back at me. Thoughts and judgments are starting to form in their minds. I can see it happening. "Sorry," I call out, laughing it off. "I'm a little out of practice!" They turn around to begin the inning.

The first batter approaches the box. I crouch, with my hands resting on my knees, the official position of a softball fielder at the ready. I find it a comforting position to be in, perhaps because it's the closest I can get to the fetal position while still looking like I'm playing softball.

Lou, a black-haired man who, at seventy-three, could still be described as "fucking enormous," approaches the plate. "He pulls to right field," says Stuart. "Don't worry about him." I relax and let my glove fall to my side. Our pitcher throws the ball toward the plate. Lou's muscles tighten and the bat lifts off his shoulder and quivers there. My heart beats out a frantic polyrhythm, and my synapses sing above it the age-old "Ballad of Left Field": "Please-God-don't-let-him-hit-it-to-me-please-God-don't-let-him-hit-it-to-me."

Our pitcher tosses one at Lou, and Lou rips it to left field. The sight of the ball hurtling toward Stuart and me appears long before the deafening boom of Bob's hit. It's only the second time anyone has hit the ball this way since I started playing. "I got it," I say quietly, hoping Stuart doesn't hear me.

"No," says Stuart, his voice quivering. "It's mine! It's coming toward me!"

"Okay!" I agree, a little too readily. But he's right—the ball is now unmistakably heading toward him.

Thanks to our having moved back before Bob hit, Stuart is perfectly placed to catch the ball. He doesn't even have to move a step—it is a routine play. Stuart gets himself in ready position. The ball hits his glove, and then, for some reason, Stuart pitches forward a bit and the softball drops onto the grass with a soft thud.

Stuart, panicking, runs after the bouncing ball as the base runners round the bases. I feel bad, but I also experience a strange and long-dormant feeling: the sense of relief and gratitude that comes when another player on your team messes up, and you're no longer alone. Later I might feel guilty about the cruelty, but on the field, I feel only pleasure.

While our team bats, I sit on the bench next to Eli the Mennonite and dread my turn at the plate. He looks more like a leprechaun than any man I've ever seen in my life—he can't weigh more than 110 pounds. "One hundred and six pounds," Eli tells me proudly, when I ask him. "I asked the doctor to help me gain weight, but the only thing that got heavier was his pocketbook!" Eli's shoulder blade sticks out so prominently it seems to be buttressing him against the bench. "Are you a Bible reader?" asks Eli. "No, not so much," I say. Eli smiles and says, "You will be." Then he turns to the field and sings a snatch from a hymn: "He prayed, but it was too late!" Eli laughs and slaps me on the back. "You know that one?"

A few minutes later I'm told that I'm up. Eli is now on base, having hit a high-bouncing chopper between first and second base. Aware that all eyes are on me, I grab a couple of bats and swing them around one-handed, like I'm considering their balance and heft. I want the bat that is least likely to give me a splinter. I go with the aluminum one. I stride to the plate and knock some dirt off my suede boots. Then I notice something remarkable, something that I have never, ever seen before in my many years of playing baseball.

The outfielders are backing out for me.

It's tremendous. The outfielders, sensing that I'm some kind of home-run-stroking wonder gorilla, have backed up farther than I've seen them back up for anyone all day. My head swells. "Hey, Rodney!" shouts one of my teammates from the first-base line. "Remember when you score to touch the white base, not the green one!" I look to my side, and notice that they've made two separate bases for the catcher and the scorer, so there are no home-plate collisions. They think I'm going to score! I think to myself. How cool is that?

The pitcher winds up and fires the ball. I try not to let myself get distracted by his "Fighting Irish" tank top, which even on an eighty-year-old is still somehow intimidating. The pitch is a terrible one, up around my eyes, so I decide not to swing. I relax and watch the ball as it drops down from eye level and lands in the center of the strike zone.

"Hey! You waitin' for one more perfect than that?" shouts the pitcher. I smile at him and take a couple practice swings, sending the message to him that I'm just letting things get interesting before I clobber one. He winds up and tosses another. It looks identical to the first—horrific, way too high, but now I'm in the throes of self-doubt. Do all good Senior League softball pitches look bad at first? So I resolve to swing at this one.

Unfortunately, Senior League softball pitches move very, very slowly, and it becomes clear after my bat has rounded perhaps a quarter of its rotation that I am way, way ahead of the ball. That requires me to dramatically slow the speed of my swing, which requires me to contort and splay my elbows. Then, as I originally thought, the pitch reveals itself to be an atrocious one, very high and inside. It's far too late to stop my motion, and I pretzel myself further to make contact with the ball. It's hideous-looking.

I graze the ball, and it dribbles to my left, into foul territory. It is now 0 and 2, and I am in great danger of striking out in my first at-bat in Senior League softball. That's when I notice the outfielders are moving in.

That's it? One ugly foul ball and now I'm not a threat? "Hey, Rodney!" shouts the shortstop Lou, one of the organizers of the league. "Get it onto the green! See if you can hit it into my mitt!" All the old-timers laugh, and I laugh along. I do an ostentatious Babe Ruth point to left field, and the left fielder moves in even closer.

The pitch comes in, and I have no choice but to swing. I can't go down on a called third strike in an old man's softball league. I wait for what seems like an outrageous amount of time for the pitch to stabilize, and I swing at it, hard. I make glorious contact, and the ball heads immediately into the dirt and then bounces at Lou the shortstop. The one who said, "See if you can hit it into my mitt!" He doesn't even have to move his glove. Lou stands there for a second, enjoying his moment of psychological victory over me. Finally he turns and tosses to the second baseman, forcing Eli out. The second baseman pivots and throws to first, and I barely beat out a double play. As I catch my breath, Lou calls out: "Hey, Rodney—thanks for listening, but I'm not on your team!" The old guys laugh. Then I hear Eli say from the dugout, "If I had his hundred sixty pounds on my body, I'd hit it a lot further than that." I'm not sure if anyone out there has ever been dissed by a peace-loving Mennonite, but does it get lower than that?

"That's all right," says the first base coach. "Good contact."

I stand on the field, hot-faced with shame, as the old-timers look at me, unimpressed—a sad waste of youth.

The next batter cracks a single into the outfield. I run to second base, and as I run, a fury erupts within me. I begin to run as fast as I can. Soon I'm like a quarter horse, hardly touching the ground, covering obscene lengths with every stride, my face scrunched into a silly mask of exertion. I want to move faster than their cataract-addled eyes could ever see. I want them to marvel at my lung capacity—33 percent greater than theirs, I've read! My legs pump hard. My footsteps kick up clouds of dust, an unmistakable smoke signal: I may be wasting my youth, but I've got plenty of it to waste.

I should have noticed that the second baseman is standing on the bag, waiting for the pickoff throw. My brain is in some sort of bloodthirsty theta state. I notice far too late, barreling into the old man at full speed. As we collide, I make a last-minute decision to try to hold his body up by the backs of his legs. That turns out to be stupid. I merely create a fulcrum by which I can trip him even more dramatically. The old man flies down into the dirt.

For an instant, I feel a bit like a WWF wrestler; I have an

almost uncontrollable urge to stand unrigged over the old man, pumping my fists together, bellowing. But then the old-timers come running in, circling around their downed friend. They take off their mitts and put their hands on him. They stare at him with eyes full of stunned, mournful concern, as if they've just watched a doe shot at point-blank range. He lies there, not moving. Suddenly I realize that I have killed the man.

For five interminable seconds, the second baseman lies there in a heap. Then, he stirs. He might be okay. I step forward, and in an act of retributive chivalry, I offer my outstretched hand to lift him up. He ignores it and stands on his own. "Watch where you're going, asshole," he says. "Haven't you ever played baseball before?" Everyone laughs and cheers, and I look over at Stuart, and bless his heart, he's not laughing.

It's the cruelest thing about sports, and probably what makes them so popular—they're very simple. You're either good or you're bad, and in the end you either win or you lose. The weak are just weak—they are a liability. It's not like civilized life, where there's spin control, the Disabilities Act, or ways to blame your failures on someone else.

When our team returns to the outfield, all I want to do is turn and grab Stuart's hand. "Why are we doing this to ourselves?" I will say to him. "This isn't us. I'm twenty-eight. You're sixty-eight. Let's leave this behind. Let's leave right now." I will take him to his house and we'll sit at tandem computers. He will write a mystery and I will check my e-mail. We'll listen to the ball game on the radio. "This is what we are," I'll tell him. "This is the kingdom that we rule, with our mighty keyboards and our royal jean shorts."

But Stuart shows up for the next game and manages to get three hits. That's why he is Chicago and I am Westchester. He is I-75, I am I-95. He is Gulf coast, and I am Atlantic coast. Stuart will stay on the softball field, like a rabbi detective still working the big-shouldered streets of Chicago after seven novels.

So I return to left field and say nothing, knowing I will retire from softball as soon as the game ends. Later, a fly ball comes my way and I catch it. It's easier once the pressure is off.

AMY BALLINGER

ON AUGUST 2, I am sitting in a car with a ninety-three-year-old woman and yelling at her. At the time, I feel quite strongly that she deserves it. And sometimes, with much older people, yelling is the only way you can get through. Without knowing the details, might you agree with me, in principle, that sometimes it's okay to yell at a ninety-three-year-old woman?

Amy Ballinger has a joke answering machine message, which is pretty impressive for a woman her age. Joke messages are a tricky art form because your callers have to hear the message repeatedly. It better be very funny. My own joke message goes: "Please leave your name and number at the beep—this call may be recorded for quality assurance purposes." It works, though it's a "thinker," in the sense that it doesn't make you laugh, but after a few seconds you think: Hey, that was funny. Amy's message is more of a red-meat, down-the-middle, capital *J* joke: "Hi, it's Amy; I'm not in," she says, in a loose, boozy drawl. "I'm out lookin' for a millionaire who takes Viagra. If I don't find one, I'll call you back." Though I think Viagra jokes are inherently cheap, I know that if our messages faced off in some kind of Answering Machine March Madness tournament, the smart money would be on Amy's message. Everyone enjoys an old lady with a joke.

A newspaper writer I met in Florida thought that a young comedy writer like myself would enjoy meeting Amy, a former stand-up comedian. So once a week, I pick Amy up at her Independent Living Facility, and we go out to lunch. She's always dressed tastefully, but when I compliment her, she says, "Shut up, I look like an old goat and you know it." The truth is, Amy is in great shape. She looks like Carol Channing in the best possible way—smiley and well put together.

Amy likes to do things for herself. Despite knee trouble, she walks without the aid of a cane or walker. She swims every day. She e-mails. In fact, she can still drive her car, very rare for a woman over ninety, though she seldom does anymore because she's scared of highway driving. When we head out for the afternoon, she introduces me to her neighbors as either her chauffeur or her drinking buddy. On the highway, she insists I drive quickly, which I find hard to do. I don't want to be the jerk who finally kills her at ninety-three years of age.

We go to a restaurant called the Grumpy Grouper and exchange stories about our lives in show business. The more time we spend together, the more I realize that we have very little in common, not even comedy. I tend to overanalyze my comedy, breaking it down into cerebral concepts like "escalations" and "misdirections." If you gave me a few hours, I could explain to you how "Why did the chicken cross the road?" deftly combines subversion, absurdity, and the "*k* sound" into a perfect joke. Amy, on the other hand, analyzes nothing. Amy is from a different school: she is just funny. Later you can't remember anything she said, but you remember laughing a lot. Sometimes at the bar, Amy will crack up everyone around the horseshoe within seconds of sitting down. Soon, she has them acting friendly, talking and goofing on one another. Amy calls this "whooping it up."

Like most comics I know, Amy will say anything to get a laugh. She isn't afraid to work blue. In fact, she's the first older woman I've ever met who I could describe as a "raunch." When she sits down for lunch she announces that her knees are bothering her. If someone offers condolences, she'll burst out laughing and say: "Yeah, my knees hurt. But what the hell, my legs still spread!"

Have you ever heard a ninety-three-year-old woman say anything like that? And the thing is, she says it a lot; "My legs still spread" is Amy's current catchphrase. The first time I heard her say it, to a three-hundred-pound black man working the desk at her community complex, I turned bright red. This is a huge guy with a very prominent gold cross around his neck. But he laughed at Amy for almost fifteen seconds, propping himself up by an elbow, the cross bouncing on the desktop as he convulsed. "My legs still spread," he kept repeating, over and over again. It's moments like that when I am a little bit in awe of Amy.

The fourth or fifth time we go out together, Amy surprises me. "My friends were asking me who I was going out with today, and I realized that I didn't even know who you are," she announces after getting into my car.

"Sure you do. You know me."

"I don't really, though. For all I know you could be some kind of rapist. You should get business cards that say who you are," she instructs me.

"Business cards that say what? 'Not a rapist'?"

"I'm just saying I don't know who you are," says Amy. We drive in silence for a minute or two, as I think about what she has said.

"Wait," I say. "So you thought to yourself, 'He could be a rapist,' and then you still got in the car?"

Amy shrugs and laughs. "Beats staying inside for the day."

In the late 1980s, Amy was drinking in a North Palm Beach bar. She had recently turned eighty. She was already the last surviving member of her family, but there were still assorted friends and lovers to whoop it up with in those days. Often, though, Amy went out alone. She'd sit at the bar and make new friends for the night. When Amy showed up that evening, the place was empty except for a group of young men laughing in a corner of the bar. Amy took an immediate interest in them. The bartender told Amy that the men were amateur stand-ups, and that the bar had hosted an open mike night that evening. Amy didn't know what any of that meant. "Oh, Amy, it's for you," the bartender said. "You should go over there and talk to that guy Richard. He organizes it." Amy walked over to Richard. Richard explained that he managed amateur stand-up nights around South Florida. If the amateur comics turn out to be any good, Richard signs them and starts finding them paying gigs.

"What do you do?" Richard asked Amy.

"I tell jokes," Amy said.

Richard looked Amy over. The hot comics at the time were people like Steven Wright and Bobcat Goldthwait, comedians with gimmicks. Wasn't being very old a pretty good gimmick?

So he told Amy that if she prepared five minutes of material, he'd put her on a stage.

In 1947, Amy found a joke book. She memorized a handful of jokes and started telling them at parties and bars. She found she had a knack for it. It was the first time in her life she remembers people telling her she was funny. This was a welcome development for Amy after an early life that she describes as "horrible from start to finish." Her father died when she was thirteen and she went right to work in a Pittsburgh laundry plant, supporting her family on seven dollars a week. Everyone she knew was dirt poor. It was a good time to be funny. Being funny didn't cost any money, and people liked to have you around.

Being funny has traditionally been men's work, and that was doubly true in the forties. Amy worked mainly with men at the plant, a situation she was fine with. "I prefer being around men," she says. "I've always understood a man's way of thinking better." But the feeling wasn't mutual. Most men she encountered resented a brash, outspoken, funny woman. So for a long time, Amy was a funny woman who couldn't be funny.

"That's so sad," I say. As soon as I say it, I know I should have seen it coming.

"Yeah," she agrees. "But what the hell. My legs still spread."

A week after Amy met Richard, she walked onstage for the first time. Against Richard's advice, she had written no material at all. She wasn't nervous until she faced the audience, and then she was petrified. She stood there for a beat, thinking about what to say. She remembers that the audience, mistaking her scared silence for comic timing, started to smile before she even said anything.

"I'm so old," she finally announced. "I should be condemned."

She got a small laugh, but most in the audience assumed that she was leading toward something bigger. Her eyes cast around the bar and settled on a large sign advertising happy hour.

"Are you enjoying happy hour?" Amy asked. "At my age, happy hour is a nap."

After her set, when the laughter had died down and another, bitter, balding comedian had taken her place onstage, Richard found Amy by the bar. "Holy shit," he said. "You killed!" For a few seconds, Amy thought that killing was a bad thing. Any comic will tell you that the secret to successful stand-up isn't just having funny things to say. It's saying things funny. There's no question that part of what made Amy say things funny was that she was an old woman. Amy had to live an entire life, work tens of thousands of days for little money, outlive four brothers, five sisters, a husband, and countless friends, but finally, at the age of eighty, she was funny.

Comedians call this "paying your dues."

Richard started booking Amy in three or four Florida comedy clubs a week, and before long, Amy was making more money than a woman in her eighties has any right to make. Local newspapers and TV stations jumped on the "old lady stand-up" and covered her extensively. She has a scrapbook full of clippings that all have the same headline: LOCAL SENIOR KEEPS 'EM LAUGHING. She had been accepted into the strange subculture of male comedians, sad young men with a strong need for a mother figure. Amy, for that matter, was happy to fill that role; she'd never had children. She said she was too busy.

"We'd sit around and say anything we wanted to each other," Amy remembers, with more emotion than I'd heard her express about anything. She even manages to wax nostalgic over Carrot Top, who was at the time an up-and-coming Florida comedian. "You should have seen him then. So young. His prop box was this big," she says, holding her hands half a foot apart.

Her act was a mix of "dirty jokes and prop comedy." She performs bits and pieces of it for me. "I'd pull out a cucumber," she tells me, "and I'd say, 'Ladies, who needs a man when you can buy cucumbers four for a dollar?' And then I'd point at the knobs on the cucumber and say, 'Men don't even have speed bumps!'"

"You said that?" I ask, a little shocked.

"People loved it," she says.

The more I think about it, the more I like her cucumber joke. It's the perfect joke for an eighty-year-old raunch to tell, combining shock value with coupon clipping. And as far as fruit-and-vegetable humor goes, it sure as hell beats hitting watermelons with sledgehammers.

By 1996, the comedy boom was over. Florida, once lousy with comedy clubs, now had only a handful left. Amy watched it happen but could do nothing. "I'd already been through one Great Depression," she says, "I didn't need to go through another."

Amy had recently moved south into an independent living facility. The facility would allow her to continue living on her own, but would provide her with three quality meals a day. If anything was to happen to her health, a nearby medical facility was included in the dues. "They just move you across the street," she says. It was a tough decision, but she was pushing ninety, and felt that the opportunity to live in a community where she'd receive closer attention at a reasonable cost was too good to pass up. She also decided to retire from stand-up comedy. It wasn't just the comedy climate. Amy's knees were beginning to bother her, and it's awfully hard to be a stand-up when you can't stand up for very long.

"Now," says Amy, "I'm the funniest person at the facility." But she admits she doesn't have much competition: "Everyone's winding down there." It's one of the first things I've heard her complain about. "Nobody likes to laugh," she says. "Nobody likes to go out. Nobody whoops it up." Sometimes she still sees her old comedy friends. One recently came by and took her to a Carrot Top show in a local arena. Amy was happy when Carrot Top remembered her.

Sitting in a bar with her, I ask Amy if she ever considers getting back into stand-up.

"Stand-up," says Amy, "now that was fun." She takes a sip and laughs. "Yep, I outlived all the fun!"

Amy's ninety-fourth birthday is coming up, and I've decided that my present to her will be a set at a comedy club. I'll have them put a chair onstage, and I'll take care of all the planning and organization. She'll love it, and it seems more appropriate than a Tower Records gift certificate, my usual go-to gift.

Finding a place for her to perform is harder than I expected. I call the few comedy clubs left, but most don't have amateur nights anymore. There aren't enough aspiring comics in the audience buying drinks to make it profitable, so they mainly book name comedians now. I downgrade and start to look for open mike nights. But they don't book comics either, only music.

"You're not paying them, so why the hell does it matter?" I say to one guy. He hangs up on me.

I get the bright idea of contacting Richard, Amy's old manager. Maybe he'd know where I can book her, and would be inclined to help out. I call Amy for his number, saying that I need to interview him. That's when I learn that Richard has won the lottery and quit the business. Finally, one day, talking to a teenager in a dingy basement coffeehouse, I ask if a ninety-four-year-old woman can perform stand-up at their entertainment night.

"Sure!" she says. "That is *adorable*."

You might want to reserve judgment on that, I think. You haven't heard the cucumber joke yet.

On the day I take Amy out for her birthday, there's the official plan and there's the secret plan. The secret plan is, of course, Amy's triumphant return to the stage. The official plan, the one Amy knows about, is for us to head up to West Palm Beach for the day so we can go see *Menopause: The Musical* at the Cuillo Centre for the Arts.

Menopause: The Musical is a smash-hit musical in South Florida that has become required viewing for every woman over the age of fifty. I am the only man in the packed theater. Amy has been excited about going, but as we drive up she admits that she does not remember her own passage through menopause. "It didn't make any impression on me," she says. *Menopause: The Musical* is two hours long and harmless enough. I could criticize it, at great length, in fact, but that would be unfair. The target audience, Amy included, loves it, singing along to the tune of "California Girls": "I wish we all could be sane and normal girls."

As we drive home, I'm trying to keep Amy in a good, positive, funny mood, but she's getting cranky as the sun goes down.

"Clever lyrics in that musical, huh?" I ask her, trying to get her back in the laughing mood. "Which was your favorite?"

"Sometimes I wish I had children," Amy responds. That seems like a red-flag conversation to me.

"My favorite was maybe when they sang 'Staying Awake'

instead of 'Staying Alive.' I guess that happens a lot. Did you ever nod off when you went through menopause?"

"Children take care of you when you get older," says Amy. "But I didn't have them. I was too busy." Amy pauses for a second. "Why are you driving so fast?" she asks me.

I take a deep breath and tell her about her new comedy gig.

"They have an open mike night in there, Amy," I tell her. "And I've arranged for you to perform."

Amy starts to squirm in the car seat. I'd expected her to resist at first and planned ways to ease her into it.

"It's going to be a pretty small crowd," I say. "Really friendly. It's a great way to get back into it."

"I don't know," says Amy.

The book *Successful Aging* had prepared me for this. "It is often difficult for older people to accept the reversal of roles in which the young become their mentors," it said. I'm ready to move into it gently, let her think it is her own idea.

"They have a chair for you," I say. "There's no shame in that. Bill Cosby does the same thing; he does sit-down now instead of stand-up."

Amy sits still, thinking for a few seconds. "No," she says. "I don't want to."

"You do want to," I tell Amy. "You always talk about how much you miss it."

"No," says Amy. She's firm about it.

I'm suddenly very angry, and I don't exactly know why. I'm irritable for some reason. Maybe it's that I haven't eaten in a while. Maybe it's that I have a bad sunburn on my back because the women in the Pool Group were talking about *The Vagina Monologues* today, and it made me too uncomfortable to ask them to rub suntan lotion on me.

"Amy," I say, louder now, "you're just feeling stage fright. You'll get over it. You've done this a thousand times."

"No," says Amy. "I want to go home. I'm tired."

Is it inevitable that everyone gives up eventually? Even someone with as much enthusiasm as Amy? What hope does that give the rest of us?

"Amy!" I'm yelling now, definitely yelling. "I set it all up! When are you going to get another chance to do this? You love stand-up!" She shakes her head. Oh God, I think, I don't want to die a comic. When comics fail onstage they call it dying. Once, a comic really did die onstage: Harry Einstein, father of Albert Brooks, at a Friars Club roast. The only way for a comic to go. Gorgeous. Away from the boredom and bedpans, in front of an audience, in the middle of a laugh. Maybe it's like dying with eighty people holding your hand.

"I never loved stand-up," she says. "It was just a kick. That's it."

I call Amy a few weeks later to apologize. I feel bad about how I acted with her. I'm not sure what got into me. God knows what kind of maniac I'll become when someone who is closer to me, like my parents, gets to be her age. I'm understanding a bit better now why so many of the elderly people I know at Century Village have strained relationships with their children. There's a lot of tension that comes from watching people you know grow old and helpless, when you want to see them as strong and capable. "You get along better with your grandchildren," one man told me, "because they expect nothing from you other than you being Grandpa."

I'm not surprised, when I next call Amy, to hear that she has changed her answering machine message.

"This is Amy," the message says, "leave a message." Then it beeps.

I leave an apology and hang up. A few days later, I get a voice mail from Amy.

"Nice to hear from you, Rodney," it says. "I'm sorry I didn't perform. The heart is willing but the body says no. Call me if you want to get some lunch and whoop it up."

So every few weeks we go to the Grumpy Grouper. I understand now: Amy doesn't need a new comedy manager. She just needs a chauffeur. Amy cracks wise from behind a plate of fried oysters and performs a sit-down set for an audience of me, while somewhere Carrot Top is selling out small stadiums. It doesn't seem right, but what the hell, her legs still spread.

SHUFFLEBOARD

For the last three days Abe hasn't been around, so we've been playing shuffleboard, just the three of us: Jimmy, Vince, and I. God, I miss Abe. He has a stabilizing effect on the rest of us because he's the sweetest man alive—tall, gentle, and with the voice of a 1940s cartoon dog. With Abe gone, Jimmy is less lovable and gets to indulge his cranky side. It's worst when it's sunny and the tennis courts next to us are full of players. Jimmy calls it "a hundred heart attacks waiting to happen." Vince, meanwhile, has become even more of a hard-ass. He's been riding me, criticizing my grasp of the rules, mechanics, and strategy of the game. I'm sorry; the *sport.* It's not a game. Don't say "game" unless you want Vince to yell at you.

I'd been showing up at the clubhouse for two weeks straight, hoping for an opening on the tennis courts. Most retirees I know play tennis, and it seemed like a sport I could dominate more easily than softball. My two athletic advantages—brute force and uncontrolled manic energy—can take you pretty far in a sport like tennis. But breaking in proved impossible. The tennis courts were always packed. In the rare event of a fill-in being needed, it became a who-you-know game, so I always ended up watching. Every day I would look over and see Jimmy, Vince, and Abe playing shuffleboard. They're the only ones playing next to nine empty shuffleboard courts. I was curious, but too many young people, when they heard I was living in Century Village, had jokingly asked whether I was playing shuffleboard. It's the big retirement community cliché. I'd long ago resolved to move beyond it.

Finally, after days of no tennis, I wandered over to the shuffleboard courts. Vince was smart. He drew back and let Abe and Jimmy engage me in conversation. They asked if I'd ever played shuffleboard and I said, "Not since I was a kid." They spoke about the sport with sincerity and eloquence: how relaxing it is, how strategic it is, how it challenges both the mind and body. It appealed to everything I'd been reading about how you age more slowly if you stay sharp physically and mentally. They made shuffleboard seem like exercise for realists.

Then they adopted a self-deprecating tone. Jimmy said that people erroneously believe that shuffleboard players are foolish and ancient, that they "have one foot in the grave and another foot on a banana peel. Grave, sure. But you see a banana peel around here?" He laughed, and I laughed, although I'm still not sure what the joke meant.

Abe and Jimmy are both in their late eighties, and Vince is in his mid-sixties. He played tennis until a leg injury forced him into a more low-impact sport. He's kind of like a former NBA player who gets injured and has to go play pro ball in Kazakhstan.

Eventually they got around to asking me if I wanted to join them for a match. I checked the action back on the tennis courts. Still too busy. It hadn't yet occurred to me that Jimmy and Abe were lifelong professional salesmen who had been laying down a sales pitch, and that now they were closing.

Jimmy and Abe spend a few minutes teaching me the rudiments of the game. They keep it simple, at first. You and your opponent take turns pushing eight molded plastic discs down a cement lane with lightweight aluminum cues. At the end of the lane there is an upside-down triangle with numbers written in it: 10, 8, 7, and –10. You're trying to land your discs in the boxes and score as many points as possible while avoiding the –10 box, which is called "the kitchen."

"You don't want to be in the kitchen," says Jimmy.

"Why is it called the kitchen?" I ask.

"I don't know. I guess 'cause what guy would want to be in the kitchen, right?"

"Lots of fellas cook today," says Abe, looking to me for approval. I nod. "My grandson, he's a great cook. Do you cook?"

"Yeah, I cook," I say.

"You're going to make some guy a great wife," says Vince. Jimmy gives Vince a dirty look.

We start. I'm teamed with Abe. Jimmy and I compete against each other on the same side of the court. The men are supportive of me, though I push the discs down the court at the same shuffleboard skill level as when I last played at the age of nine.

"Nice shot!"

"Good form!"

"This kid's a natural!"

The adoration takes its toll. I begin to feel like some sort of shuffleboard Tiger Woods, a prodigy with incredible latent talent for the sport, phenomenal "disc sense." I feel this way despite the fact that I'm scoring negative points.

While Jimmy and I wait for the others to finish their round, he curses the tennis club.

"They have, what, two, three hundred members? Everyone wants to play tennis. The shuffleboard club used to have hundreds of members." Jimmy points to an athletic-looking man on a far tennis court. "You know who that is?" he says. "That's Max. The president of the Shuffleboard Club. Even *he* plays tennis. They're all over there now, running around like idiots." Jimmy is right about that. The elderly people are exerting themselves over there on the courts. The men in particular appear to think that they're on the pro tour, although tour tennis players wouldn't, I think, wear black socks with their tennis shoes.

I'm remembering a walk I took with my grandfather. We passed a shuffleboard court and I asked him if he ever played. "No," he said, outraged, "shuffleboard is for old people." I found this a peculiar notion coming from an eighty-one-year-old. It appears that the newest wave of retirees, the young-old, are, at the age of sixty-five, rebelling against their parents, the old-old. One gerontologist, Bernice Neugarten, has written a lot about the conflict. Young-old people don't want to do old-old-people things. They won't be caught dead playing shuffleboard, since, to them, shuffleboard *is* death. So now shuffleboard is dying off. Tennis is king.

"If it doesn't appeal to young people, the sport is kaput," says Jimmy. "It's a shame. You sure have a knack for it, though." At this point what's going on is crystal clear. They have plans for me, these old-old guys. I'm some kind of Baby Shuffleboard Moses. They want to beget me, swaddle me, place me in a bulrush basket, and send me downriver to the Tennis Pharaoh.

To my surprise, I find this idea appealing, in a *Last of the Mohicans* kind of way. I like the gravitas of being responsible for carrying the sport forward. I like the fact that I seem so important to these guys. But most of all, I like the idea of becoming the best in the world at a sport. It seems like an attainable-enough goal, even for me. Even after the softball debacle. Nobody else my age plays shuffleboard. Once the current generation of players passes on, I'll be the best by default. Plus, if old people can be good at shuffleboard, how difficult can the sport be?

"We play every day," says Abe, after we've finished up.

"You should join the club," says Jimmy.

"I can join the club?"

"Sure! We'd be happy to have you."

"Okay," I say. "I'm in."

"Then pay up," says Vince. He extends his hand. "Eight dollars' initiation fee."

I turn to Jimmy and Abe. One would think that Baby Shuffleboard Moses gets his initiation fee waived.

"You get four free breakfasts," says Jimmy.

I believe salesmen call that the bait and switch.

Next time I show up for shuffleboard, the fun is over. The men are done coddling me. It's not unlike in *An Officer and a Gentleman*, but I'm the only private and there's three Lou Gossett Jr.'s determined to break my spirit. Needless to say, it turns out that shuffleboard is more than just shoving a disc around with a stick. It is a game with—no, I'm sorry, Vince—a *sport* with a tremendous number of rules. I won't bore you with most of them, but two things you should know are: 1) The regulation shuffleboard court must be exactly fifty-two feet long, and 2) You don't lean on the shuffleboard cue fork-side-down, because then everyone yells at you.

Most days we scrimmage, and it's frustrating. Vince mutters and yells at me. Jimmy is more patient. His whole thing is you have to keep doing it until you internalize it. The short-left-step-long-right-step, the flick at the end of the push so you get the "finesse." Finesse wins and loses matches. Jimmy played for years before he improved to the point of finesse.

"You gotta stick with it," says Abe. "I didn't hit my peak until I was probably seventy-eight or seventy-nine."

I stick with it and try hard to get better. I take shuffleboard strategy books out of the library, full of black-and-white photographs of 1950s shuffleboarders demonstrating proper form, their slacks way too snug around their abdomens. Sometimes I come back to the courts late in the afternoon and practice on my own. It doesn't seem to have any impact. I continue to get my twenty-eight-year-old ass sent to the kitchen.

Abe leaves for a trip to New York in early November, and then, one morning, a new guy shows up. His name is Sam, he's in his late eighties, and it's the first time he's ever come to the shuffleboard courts.

"My wife told me, 'Get out of the condo—or else!' " says Sam. Vince and Jimmy, spotting a new recruit, immediately start selling the guy on the benefits of regular shuffleboard play. Since Abe isn't around, I wonder if I'm supposed to join in.

"It's a good sport," I tell Sam. "It's got strategy."

We split into two teams. Vince is my teammate, and Sam is my opponent. He says he's played shuffleboard before up North, but he seems to have no idea what he's doing. He lines up the black and yellow discs in a jumble, without alternating them by color. I sort them out and eye him down.

"My wife told me to get out of the condo—or else!" says Sam again. Now that I've had some one-on-one time with Sam, I see that he has an unfocused look in his eyes. "Shuffleboard. Good exercise," he says. "My wife told me to get out of the condo or else."

I'm starting to get the very strong impression that Sam might not be all there. This is always a sad thing, something

I've yet to get used to even after several months among elderly people. The doctors behind the MacArthur Study on Aging took pains to point out that loss of mental clarity is not as inevitable as many senior citizens believe. Only 10 percent of senior citizens have Alzheimer's. The rest can expect a little deterioration of their mental abilities and short-term memory, but nothing major. Abe and Jimmy are perfect examples, two men, almost ninety, who are as sharp as they've ever been.

But after I notice that Sam is probably not all there, I'm not thinking about any of those things. What I'm thinking is: Finally, somebody I can beat at shuffleboard.

Sam plays with no strategy. He doesn't utilize "St. Pete's pilots" or try to knock me in the kitchen. Each shot is more random than the last. Consequently, I am annihilating him on the court. I'm making shot after shot. My shuffleboard cue has ceased to feel like a shuffleboard cue and feels instead like some sort of musket or mighty staff. I am merciless. I am destroying. The cool early-morning wind is at my back; the sun, still low on the horizon, creates a warming glow around my body. Despite my bad posture, I know I look like a god to Sam.

This doesn't stop my teammate, Vince, from keeping up a steady stream of criticism of my strategic play. He thinks that I'm shooting my discs from the wrong part of the court, resulting in lousy angles. Just to spite Vince, I continue doing exactly that.

By the third round, I'm starting to feel bad. Sam is spending so much time in the kitchen, he should be getting paid minimum wage. Maybe I should be letting this poor guy win. Perhaps he has been through enough. As it happens, I don't have to let him win. Vince's constant criticism has jangled my nerves and now I'm messing up my shots. Somehow my addled opponent and I begin to tie, and then he begins to pull ahead.

"He's blowing it!" Vince keeps muttering to Jimmy, as if I can't hear him from fifty-two feet away.

"Geez Louise," says Sam, before putting eight more unanswered points on the board. "He sure takes this serious. It's just a game."

"It's not a game," I say. "It's a sport."

I try to focus. Cross pilot. St. Pete. Knock his points, block my points. Loosen my grip. Short-left-step-long-right-step. Push with my body. Flick the wrist for finesse. This is how shuffleboard is played.

I land myself in the kitchen. I notice that all of a sudden the air has become humid. Goddamn Florida.

"I told him that was a shitty angle," Vince whispers to Jimmy.

"I can hear you, Vince," I say, the anger rushing out of me. "It doesn't make it any easier when you're criticizing every shot."

"If you listened to me," shouts Vince, "you wouldn't be mucking it up!"

"Hey!" yells Jimmy. "Easy, easy!"

Sam takes a step away from the court. "Great, guys," he says, as if he's oblivious to what's happening. "I think that's it for me."

Vince whips toward Sam. "What? We're in the middle of a match."

"You guys take this too serious," he says.

"They're just playing around," says Jimmy.

"I don't take it so serious," says Sam. "I just do it for fun. It's good exercise. I'm goin' home now."

"I thought your wife told you to get out of the condo or else," Vince says. Sam looks at him like he's crazy. He lays his cue along the bench. "Okay, fellas," he says. "Take care now."

I keep thinking about how Abe says he didn't reach his shuffleboard peak until his late seventies. More and more I am accepting that I won't be able to properly play the sport until forty years from now. I don't think it's possible for a young man to slow down enough to master the sport of shuffleboard. You have to wait till the point where it's just too much energy to try hard, and then the Spirit of Shuffleboard fills you, and you're ready to kick some butt.

Once I realize that, it is a lot harder to drag myself out of bed at six forty-five to slide a piece of plastic around. But for some reason I still show up. The sport has kind of grown on me, and I feel some weird obligation to those guys.

While I am on the court the other day, I get a call on my cell phone from my friend Jenni in Los Angeles. She says she hasn't heard from me in a while, and I realize she is right, I have been calling home a lot less frequently. Jenni complains that she has been working a lot of late nights lately on a television show.

Then she changes the subject, starts asking me what I am up to down in Florida. Does she sound jealous?

It is a funny thing to hear on a workday morning, as I stand on the courts with the shuffleboard guys, watching the rising sea of tennis players in front of us. The shuffleboard tournament is starting soon, and I am going to be there. For the first time in a while, I actually feel useful. I am going to part that sea of tennis players and help save shuffleboard.

BEEP

I AM HAPPY TO ANNOUNCE that the parrot outside my room has learned to say something new. Its repertoire is no longer confined to the phrase "Not to worry!" and an impression of my alarm clock. The parrot, in fact, has decided to bestow a great honor on me. It has decided to start imitating me.

I didn't train the parrot to do this. I make a point of ignoring the parrot. Never spoke to it. No, the parrot took the initiative on this one. It spent several months listening to me as I went about my life. Certainly it heard me say many things, but it has determined, apparently, that I can best be summed up with one phrase. That phrase is this: "Hey man, what's up?"

That, according to the parrot, is what I am all about. "Hey man, what's up?" It picked this up, I am certain, by listening to me talk on the phone. That is my typical phone greeting when talking to Eva, Nick, Jenni, and Jill: "Hey man, what's up?" It is gender nonspecific.

What's particularly irritating is how well the parrot says it. In a good impersonation, the outright accuracy is less important than the nuances. The parrot is making fun of me, after all, and all the little touches are perfect. It captures exactly my hoarse, nasal speaking voice. The parrot nails my intonation, the way I always say the last syllable in up-speak.

To have a bird distill your entire existence down to four words is something I would wish on nobody. It's harrowing to face how right the bird is. And then you begin to inwardly beg the bird to learn another phrase, anything to make you seem deeper, more multifaceted. But you don't want to appear to want it too much, because the bird can sense that.

"I can barely hear you," says Jill, as we talk on the phone one evening. "Why are you whispering?"

"I am whispering," I say, "because the bird is listening."

"Oh God," she says. "This is sad. Are all retired people like you?"

I'm no longer afraid to talk to the parrot. I talk to him all the time now. Of course, he never adds any of these new phrases to the rotation. He seems quite satisfied with his repertoire as it stands. Creative people can be like that, clinging steadfastly to the purity of their own vision and unwilling to collaborate, unwilling to evolve.

"Hey man, what's up?" the parrot says.

"Shut up, you douche-bag bird," I say. I look at the painting of Jesus and I shrug without apology. If He lived with the bird, He'd go nuts too.

THE FUTURE OF THE SPORT

I'M WALKING IN THE CLUBHOUSE PARKING LOT one afternoon, when I run into Abe from the Shuffleboard Club. I didn't recognize him; you put a baseball cap on an old man, and he somehow becomes a different guy.

"Hey! Rodney!" he shouts. "You haven't been by the courts in a while!"

"Yeah, I've been a little busy, Abe."

"The tournament starts next Monday!" says Abe. "We need sixteen players! Are you coming for the tournament?"

I thought I was ready for the shuffleboard tournament, but lately I've been having second thoughts. The Century Village shuffleboard tournament takes four months. It requires you to show up three days a week, Monday-Wednesday-Friday. Colossal time commitment. I've seen how intense these guys can get about shuffleboard practice, so I can only imagine. If I missed a match, Vince might actually beat me to death.

"I don't think I'm coming," I tell Abe. My thinking is that if I lower expectations from the beginning, I'll be able to attend the shuffleboard games at my leisure.

"You're not coming? Why not? Aren't you a club member?"

"Yes."

"You should come, then. It's the big thing we do, the tournament. Everyone comes!"

Abe's lip quivers a bit. It could be from emotion, or just one of those quivers that old men's lips do sometimes. Why did it have to be Abe I ran into? Why not Vince or Jimmy? Jimmy is almost as sweet a guy as Abe, but has a crabbier face, a little easier to say no to. With Abe, it's different. He's such a well-intentioned guy. It would be like having to shoot a St. Bernard in the head as it happily sniffs the muzzle of your rifle.

I sigh. "What time do I have to be there, Abe?" He pats my shoulder a few times and I think, Oh, great, now I'm the dog.

I show up to the tournament two minutes late, on purpose, as a very conscientious objection. It doesn't seem to register, though. It's bedlam on the shuffleboard courts, in the relative sense. There are twelve club members gathered already. When have I ever seen more than three people here? Abe and Vince, meanwhile, strut around, showing me off to the other members. I've never seen Abe and Vince so juiced up; they're acting like the mayors of Shuffletown. "This is the camaraderie of the sport," Jimmy tells me. "This is why we do this."

Twenty minutes later, there are still thirteen of us, which I should have recognized as an omen. Everyone has sat down on the benches lining the courts, silent and glum. That strikes me as another bad omen, like cows lying down in grass before a lightning storm.

"This is terrible," says Jimmy. "This has never happened before."

"I'm sure people are still coming," I offer. But I don't believe this. Elderly people may be slow-moving, but in my experience they are punctual.

On Wednesday, we field ten players. We wait around for half an hour and then we go home. On Friday, there are eight. We wait for forty-five minutes and go home. Morale hits a new low. Someone's going to stick a shuffleboard cue in an electrical socket and end it all one of these days.

On Monday, I lie in bed until the last possible minute, then go. That day it's just me, Abe, Vince, and Jimmy again. We wait an hour, not even mentioning the tournament, and then Vince makes me scrimmage and kicks my ass.

"Who are all these people?" I ask Abe.

There are at least one hundred people at the Shuffleboard Club Welcome Back Election Breakfast. "They're members," says Jimmy.

"Yeah, but . . . where have they been for the last two weeks?"

"A lot of people belong to clubs for the free food," says Abe. "It's a good deal for them. They pay eight bucks annual membership, and they get three or four free meals out of it."

"That's outrageous," I say. "How can you guys stand for that?"

Jimmy shrugs. It's a basic thing that elderly people don't question. You join clubs to get free food.

A muscular-looking seventy-five-year-old stands up in front of the crowd and begins to speak. It's a few seconds before I realize that it's Max, the Shuffleboard Club president. I've never seen him up close before. He has a wiry, compact body with excellent muscle tone. Max is notorious in the Shuffleboard Club for preferring tennis to shuffleboard. He hasn't come by the courts for months.

"Hey, folks," shouts Max. He has the boozy air of someone who has called thousands of meetings to order. "First, let me just say—welcome back to sunny Florida!"

This garners a big laugh, because it's raining outside. Classic shitty opening joke. I feel my fists beginning to clench.

"The bagels will be out in a minute," announces Max. "Two free bagels for everyone. You want a third, you gotta slide five dollars in my pocket!" Everyone in the crowd laughs. I can't believe how mad this makes me. Here I am, getting up early three days a week and then this guy gets to waltz in at the last minute and be Mr. Funny Guy Bagel Man?

Shuffleboard was founded in the fifteenth century. Back then it was often played on an actual board, using coins as playing pieces. The coins were called groats. The groats were shoved by hand or shovel so that they came to a stop within a marked scoring area. It was called shovel-groat, and sometimes shovel-board. Shuffleboard, the modern term, was popularized aboard cruise ships at the turn of the century. I thought about cruise ships as I sat there at the Shuffleboard Club bagel breakfast. Then I thought about cruise ship viruses, and then icebergs. Then I thought about the way the *Titanic* created a vacuum when it went down, sucking everyone underwater.

Then the bagel plate made it to me, Jimmy, and Abe, and all that was left was pumpernickel, which somehow seemed like the perfect bagel for the moment.

Shuffleboard has a public relations problem. That's crystal clear at this point. Has a single shuffleboard championship event been broadcast on any of the twelve thousand ESPN channels?

Has a single shuffleboard player been featured on the cover of *Sports Illustrated* or in one of those Gatorade commercials sweating that weird green stuff?

After the shuffleboard breakfast, I find Lenny, the shuffleboard club member in charge of flyers. I'm not sure what this duty entails, exactly, since I've never seen a single shuffleboard flyer.

"Lenny," I say, "how would you like some help with flyers?"

"Some help with what?"

"Shuffleboard flyers. You're in charge of them."

"Oh yeah," he says, as if recalling some long-forgotten fact. "That would be great!"

Every morning, Max the Shuffleboard Club president shows up at the tennis courts at five to eight. He has three outfits that he seems to alternate, all more or less the same: plain white shorts and a shirt striated with a primary color and hugging his gut. Max plays tennis intensely, but not intensely enough to overcome the fact that he runs like a penguin. I've been watching him for a few mornings, filling a notebook with the corny jokes he shouts out to his fellow players while they hit the ball around.

"Are you trying to test my mettle?" he shouts. "I coulda told you I was made of aluminum!"

After a few days, I conclude my fact-gathering and approach the man. "Hi," I say. "You're Max, right?"

"Yeah," he says warily.

"I'm writing something about the community," I say, hoping to quickly disarm him. "Could I interview you about the Tennis Club?"

"Oh, yeah! Sure!" he says. He motions to the other men. "This fella's gonna interview me. I'm gonna be famous!"

"Tell me about the Tennis Club," I say. "It looks pretty popular."

"Oh, sure," he says. "We got three hundred, four hundred members. Very popular."

"Uh-huh." I scribble "400" on my pad. "And you're the president of the Shuffleboard Club too, right?"

Max looks around to see if anybody has overheard, then steps closer to me.

"Yeah," he says, in more of a gesture than a word.

"I bet the Shuffleboard Club is really popular too," I say.

"Yeah. Very popular." He nods. I nod. I say nothing. "Maybe not as popular," he adds. "Hundred fifty maybe."

"Boy oh boy," I say, "you must be busy, playing tennis and shuffleboard all the time."

"I like to be active, to exercise," he says, sounding apologetic all of a sudden. "A lot of people today, that's what they want, exercise."

"They've been having a lot of trouble with the shuffleboard tournament," I say. "Not enough players. Or something."

Max takes another step closer to me. "You know . . . tennis, it's more prestigious. It's a prestige sport."

I take notes, saying nothing. He feels compelled to continue. "People change their interests," he says. "I'm sure you know that."

"Right. People change . . . interests. Got it."

I continue scribbling, looking up every once in a while to smile at Max, who is beginning to squirm.

Max shows up for the next tournament day, in his tennis clothes. "Take a look! We got customers today!" Jimmy shouts to me, motioning at Max with obvious pleasure.

We begin to scrimmage. Max is out of practice, and Jimmy is unsparing. Every time he knocks one of Max's shots into the kitchen, Jimmy grins and shouts out, "El Presidente!"

At nine, the tennis courts let out and the players begin to

file past the shuffleboard courts with amused looks on their sweaty faces.

"Is that you, Max?" one asks.

"You play shuffleboard, Max?" another asks.

"Me? Well . . ." Max looks around at us, then back at them. I'm reminded of a high school lunchroom, of a former geek caught by his football buddies eating lunch with his nerdy old friends. After several false starts, Max manages to stammer out a sentence.

"I play every once in a while . . . 'cause . . . the tennis courts were so full today . . . I didn't want to wait, that's all."

"You fellas interested in playing shuffleboard?" asks Abe, oblivious to it all.

"No," one says, his face scrunching up. "It's not my thing."

They walk on. "See you tomorrow!" shouts Max after them, but they don't answer. Welcome back to the Shuffleboard Club, Max.

I put on a pot of coffee and start writing shuffleboard flyers. Simple, edgy, funny, attention-grabbing. This was my mandate.

DO YOU LIKE FUN?
COME PLAY SHUFFLEBOARD!

This is plainly not good. I'm just warming up.

COME CATCH SHUFFLEBOARD FEVER!
(SHUFFLEBOARD FEVER MAY NOT
BE COVERED BY MEDICARE)

That one, I feel, is funny but maybe a little subtle. So I decide to leave subtlety behind and employ one of advertising's oldest tricks: lying outright.

SHUFFLEBOARD! THE FASTEST-GROWING SPORT IN AMERICA!

SHUFFLEBOARD! THE MOST POPULAR SPORT IN THE WORLD!

I print them out and lay them in the "good" stack.

Then I begin to think about celebrity endorsements. My gut feeling is that celebrities won't bother to sue me if I appropriate their names to promote a shuffleboard club in South Florida.

"SHUFFLEBOARD IS THE BEST WAY I KNOW TO MEET PEOPLE ."
—STAR OF TELEVISION AND FILM PAUL NEWMAN

"WHENEVER I PLAY SHUFFLEBOARD, I MAKE NEW FRIENDS."
—SINGER MANDY PATINKIN

"PLAYING SHUFFLEBOARD IS THE SINGLE MOST EXCITING THING I HAVE DONE IN MY LIFE."
—LUNAR ASTRONAUT NEIL ARMSTRONG

My friend Nicholas hooks me up with Randy Van Cleek, one of New York's top young advertising guys. He's responsible for, among many other things, a series of award-winning Sony commercials featuring a little blue alien. Randy seems to be an easygoing, open-minded guy, so I ask him to come on board as an unpaid consultant to help me sell shuffleboard to the Century Village population.

"I've never really targeted anything toward senior citizens," says Randy. "Advertising tends to ignore old people. A buddy of mine once did a campaign for a stool loosener. Explosive bowel syndrome, that kind of thing. That's probably the closest I've gotten to it."

I explain to Randy that it doesn't matter that he has no experience. I want to tap into his hip, edgy style, which might appeal to young-old people who still think they're old-young people. "Oh," says Randy. He thinks for a bit. "Here's the thing," he says. "It's not just strengthening shuffleboard. It's weakening its enemies. You want to go after tennis hard. Superhard. Take tennis out at the knees."

DID YOU KNOW: TENNIS PLAYERS ARE 450% MORE LIKELY TO HAVE A HEART ATTACK THAN SHUFFLEBOARD PLAYERS?

SHUFFLEBOARD: IT'S HEART SMART.

TENNIS IS GREAT EXERCISE. IF YOU CONSIDER EXERCISE GETTING LIFTED INTO THE BACK OF AN AMBULANCE WITH ACUTE DEHYDRATION.

SHUFFLEBOARD: THE SAFE SPORT.

November 18: The first day the Shuffleboard Club draws over sixteen people to a tournament day. We begin to play our first official match, and then the clouds roll in and the raindrops begin to fall. It might as well be raining frogs. We all go home. Does God hate shuffleboard?

* * *

December 3: It is so strange, Jimmy has to count three times: seventeen shuffleboard players have shown up, for no discernible reason. No phone calls have been made. No new ads have been posted. There are no free bagels.

"Okay, then," says Jimmy, sounding shocked. "Let's make some teams."

As many hours as I've spent here, it is the first time I've ever experienced true shuffleboard in action. When the tournament starts rolling, and the adrenaline is kicking in, you start to feel kind of badass. Kind of like a "pool shark," except you're a "shuffleboard shark." Now that I think about it, that doesn't sound as cool.

I compete against an eighty-year-old woman, Lois, who mops the court with me. That's something I've come to like about shuffleboard: It's one of the only sports I can think of where age or sex has little bearing on ability. That said, I feel it's only fair that I get a small revenge on Lois by mentioning here that she is stout and has short hair, and reminds me, physically, of several female school-bus drivers I've had.

"What did I tell ya!" shouts Jimmy from his court. "It's fun, shuffleboard! You havin' fun?"

"Yeah, yeah," I say. "Fun!"

"Future of the sport," says Jimmy, pointing at me with his cue. "The future!" He will go on to win the whole tournament, or at least its four official playing days.

Many months later, I host a shuffleboard party for people my age in Los Angeles. I send out about forty e-mail invitations, but somehow when the day comes only five people have agreed to show up.

The only public shuffleboard court I can locate in the Los Angeles area is down in El Segundo. This is a corporate and industrial wasteland most famous for its enormous oil refinery, located under LAX's southbound flight zone. A sign next to the refinery says: WARNING: EXPOSURE TO AIR IN OR NEAR REFINERY MAY BE HAZARDOUS TO YOUR HEALTH. I have to laugh. It's for sure: God hates shuffleboard.

The Parks Department supplies us with shuffleboard equipment that looks like it hasn't been used in decades; the discs look more like chew toys. Two players drop out at the last moment, so there are three of us. That isn't enough to play, so I start accosting the baggy-short-wearing skate kids around us to see if we can find some more players.

"Anyone want to play shuffleboard?!" Try saying that to fourteen-year-olds and not feeling like a goober.

"No thanks . . . we're good," they say.

"Come on!" I say. "It's just like skateboarding, but with less skating and more shuffling!"

My companions, to my amazement, seems to like shuffleboard. They love the shuffleboard lingo: "the kitchen," "the Tampa pilot," "sucker bait." At the end of the day, as the odd crimson sunset spreads out over the oil refinery, things feel both hopeful and toxic. Everyone even says they'd like to do it again, and deep down I know that shuffleboard is not going to die and I feel happy about that.

On a side note, although nobody but me has ever played shuffleboard before, I'm still beaten soundly. It's kind of embarrassing after all the trash I talked.

YOKO

A FEW MONTHS FROM NOW my twin sister is getting married, and I have more or less given up on bringing a date. It's dispiriting because, as the twin brother of the bride, I feel there is a quiet expectation that we should be in the same place. I should at least be engaged by now. And if I'm not engaged, if I'm lagging a bit behind (and in fairness, I was born five minutes after her), I am, at the minimum, supposed to be part of a "You're next!" type couple. That's the couple everyone walks up to at a wedding and says "You're next!" to while wagging their finger at them.

My situation is not just bad luck. I am, I admit, very picky. The problem I am facing now, in the retirement community, is that I am a picky person with nobody to pick. My opportunities for finding a Hail Mary wedding date here are nil. Vince, the cantankerous guy I know in the Shuffleboard Club, offered to set me up with his twenty-five-year-old niece, Haley. She is staying with him for a few months "figuring things out." It seemed to have some potential. Several weeks later I followed up on it and he informed me that Haley had turned lesbian and gone to work at the local Home Depot. I consider going by the store and inviting her to the wedding anyway. At least then people might be less concerned about whether we're "next!" and more concerned as to why my wedding date is wearing burlap coveralls.

My primary goal, then, has become less about finding a date and more about forgetting the situation. It's been easy. I haven't checked in with my friends back home or talked to my parents or sister in weeks. If you ever want to avoid anything unpleasant, I recommend you move to Florida and try out retirement early. People back home will think you fell off the face of the earth. They have such an aversion to thinking about getting older that they will believe you when you tell them that satellite coverage is bad down here because elderly retirees don't have cell phones.

I've been taking long drives by myself lately. Not to the ocean anymore, but west now, to the edge of the Everglades swampland, where development ends, as the Top 40 on Y100 serenades me with the same Craig David song every fifteen minutes, in which the singer is introduced to a girl on a Monday, "*took her for a drink on Tuesday, we were making love by Wednesday.*"

Jesus, I sigh, my radio's going to have more grandchildren than me.

I have redoubled my efforts to spend time with my elderly retiree neighbors. Specifically, I am trying to spend even more time with elderly women. Natural intuition would tell you that young men and old men would make better buddies, but that hasn't been my experience. Whenever I spend time with old men, I am reminded of my shortcomings. They're always talking about how they stormed Normandy or contributed to V-E Day. Then they always want to know why I'm not up North earning money. If I complain to them about not being happy with my career, they don't seem to identify. Who's happy with their career? And when it comes to romance, many old men get way more action than me, and they won't shut up about it. Or they get no action, and think I'm a waste of a young penis. Then they won't shut up about that.

"You should be fighting off the women!" they say. That's the kind of thing you get sick of hearing every day. Old men are accomplished, pragmatic, and obsessed with sex; they're lousy company if you're lonely.

I have far more in common with old women than old men. A lot of them have lost their spouse, so they're single just like me. I read on the U.S. Department of Health and Human Services website that nearly half of all the women over sixty-five in the United States are widows. There are nearly 700,000 new ones every year. Also, like me, they are picky. Their only real romantic options are old men, and they often find it hard to get excited about them because, as my friend Lee says, "they all seem like old men." Also, older women are not obsessive about sex and romance like older men are. They don't spend every hour of the day griping about their situation or bird-dogging men. They seem mellow about it; they're far more likely to talk about orthopedics.

Here's what I've learned by observing elderly women. During the day, elderly women seem to keep to themselves and run errands. If I visit a supermarket before noon, you can be sure there will be a hundred women in there examining cans for dents. The weird thing is that in their universe, dents are good, because you can make a scene at checkout and browbeat an overworked teenager into giving you a discount. He will, just to keep the line moving. I have found that elderly women don't respond well when you approach them while they're shopping. It's like approaching a bear while it's eating. In the afternoon, the women, satiated from their morning shopping, often settle down for a canasta game. They'll let men watch canasta but they won't let them play; it's the elderly version of jumping rope or hopscotch.

Nighttime is when things get most difficult. I can only spend so many consecutive nights trolling around Borders bookstore with a copy of *The Lovely Bones* under my arm, hoping a local girl strikes up a conversation with me. Nighttime is when I feel I can most benefit from some soothing, restorative elderly woman accompaniment, and at night, a lot of elderly women play bingo.

One of the most popular bingo halls in the area is hidden inside a forgotten strip mall set back from Atlantic Avenue. It is unmarked and lined with mirrored windows so you can't see in. It seems more suited to an illegal bookie operation, or a sleeper cell. The only other operating business in the horseshoe is a prosthetics store. I can't imagine anyone would know the store exists, so my hunch is they must exclusively service women who lose their arms while playing bingo. Inside, there are two hundred grandmothers in one room, wearing Christmas sweaters, slacks, and slip-on sneakers. It looks like a geriatric, recreational version of the Triangle Shirtwaist Factory. The women are perched at long cafeteria-style tables picking at fried buffet food and waiting for the game to begin. I'm not sure what kind of pheromones two hundred grandmothers give off, but whatever it is, this bingo room has been trapping them for years. After a few minutes I am relaxed and can hardly remember what was stressing me out. Why didn't I come here sooner?

I buy some bingo sheets, sit down, and am engaged in a conversation with Hannah, a retired schoolteacher across the table. She's very kind and talkative. I remind Hannah of her son, who I soon discover is a married, fifty-year-old firefighter in north Michigan. Other women at nearby tables turn around and join in our talk. They love that I'm here. Everyone seems to be a retired schoolteacher. That would explain the vibe of the place, which is somewhere between a teachers' lounge and an OTB.

The bingo game begins. I've played bingo a few times before, at summer camp and whatnot. It's harmless, fun, and passes the time. What I soon learn, though, is that elderly women in South Florida play bingo on an altogether different level. It is hard-core. Everyone stops talking. I'm used to playing one bingo card at a time, but these women play at least three or more. Their agile hands dance over their pages, with a dexterity honed by decades of grading papers and forwarding film strips.

The bingo numbers are called at a blazing speed. There is no margin for error; you have to frantically find your numbers as fast as you can. I'm using a ballpoint pen to mark called numbers. Apparently that's against the Bingo Code, because after the first game begins Hannah the retired schoolteacher becomes enraged. "You need a dabbah!" she says. Her accent becomes more pronounced when she's angry. It fills me with a shameful kindergarten feeling, like I forgot to bring a mat to naptime.

Soon, the other women turn around, as if they all share one group mind.

"Why don't you have a dabbah!" they shout. "Go get a dabbah!"

A dabbah turns out to be a dabber, a large Magic Marker you use to dab ink onto the bingo card. It costs one dollar.

"Did they chaahge you?" Hannah shouts when I sit down. "The dabbah comes free with the game!"

"Don't pay!" they all shout. "It's free! Go get youah dollah back!"

I get my dollar back. A minute later I offend the bingo gods again, because apparently I have neglected to buy a Pink Speedy.

"Why don't you have a Pink Speedy?!" they shout.

"I don't know what that is," I say.

"You need a Pink Speedy!" they shout. "Go get a Pink Speedy!"

A Pink Speedy turns out to be a special bingo bonus game. As for the other bingo games we play, I am at a loss. I have no idea how to play Hatpin. I don't know when I've got a "Postage" pattern. And it has shocked me to see how much the bingo-playing has transformed the elderly women I am playing with. They're cranky and even potty-mouthed. They say things like "Where are the fuckin' *O*'s?" These are former schoolteachers. These are women who used to make me put pennies in the cursing jar. "Why aren't you playing?" they all want to know after I've given up. "You fell behind! You can't keep up?"

Why are they jumping all over me? Who cares if I'm not playing bingo right? I'm outraged, but part of me likes what's happening. It's a sick thrill to be getting so much attention from so many women at once.

After bingo, almost everyone disperses. But one woman approaches me to ask me my name. She's a retired schoolteacher named Patty, with a stout build and brown hair in a bowl haircut. The conversation turns awkward when I ask Patty when she retired, and she says, "I retired when one of my students shot me twice in the chest with a gun."

* * *

The Not for Women Only Club is not for women only. As far as I can tell, though, I am the only male dues-paying member. Nobody seems to mind when I come to the meetings and sit quietly, even when we're discussing girl things like "Menopause Memories" or playing games like "Know Your Heart Wheel of Fortune." It was at the Not for Women Only Club that a woman named Ruby first suggested that I invite a friend as a date to my sister's wedding.

"You must have some female friends you could bring."

"I do, but most of them are married," I say.

"But not all?"

"No, not all, but . . ."

I trail off, but I know what I would have said: Bringing a friend is admitting defeat. I might as well bring my sister as a date to her own wedding. At least if I go alone I am taking some sort of a stand.

I also join the Art Appreciation Club. It seems like the perfect version of what I am looking for. The club is all women, and is active but noncompetitive. We all walk around looking at art, appreciating it. It gives us something to talk about. The perfect distraction from our love lives. Also, it seems less likely that an elderly woman will yell at me.

My first Art Appreciation Club outing occurs on a Saturday morning. Our trip leader steps to the front of the bus and tells us where we're going: the Museum of Contemporary Art in Miami, not far from where my grandmother used to live when I visited as a kid. That's going to be a two-hour bus trip, which produces some grumbling. Then the leader tells us about the art we will be seeing. We are going to an exhibit called "Yes." It is devoted to the works of Yoko Ono. That is shocking to me. Does anyone on this bus even know who Yoko Ono is?

"Yoko Ono," says my bus seatmate. "I believe she is some sort of Japanese artist."

* * *

The guide at the museum is acting like she drew the short straw by getting our group this morning. “Yoko Ono is not an artist per se,” she says, and I can see looks of confusion form on the faces of the club members. Not an artist? Then what will we appreciate? “She was more interested in concepts than art,” says the guide. “Do you remember the hippies? Yoko was part of that community. She is arguably the most famous widow in the world.”

That fact seems to get everyone’s attention.

“She was married to John Lennon,” the guide continues, “who was shot in 1980. Does everyone here know John Lennon?”

Most of our hands go up.

“You see,” says our trip leader, “we’re not as old as you think!”

“Oh no,” says our guide, “you are very much Yoko’s contemporaries. She just turned seventy years old.”

We sit down in a small theater and start to watch some of Yoko’s films. The first is a thirty-minute film consisting of nothing but tight shots of various naked buttocks.

“Yoko called this film *Intelligent Bottoms,*” says our guide. “She was trying to show how similar everyone is when you look at their underside.”

We sit and watch the naked buttocks. After a few minutes, some of the women leave. Others try to tough it out. The woman sitting next to me evaluates each pair of buttocks as they appear on the screen.

“That’s a nice tushy,” she says. “That one’s a nice tushy too . . . that’s a big tushy . . . that’s a nice tushy. Isn’t that a nice tushy?”

“Yes,” I say, not knowing what else to say. “That’s a nice tushy.”

The next film we watch features shots of several flies walking all over a woman's naked body, including her pubic hair and breasts. Yoko Ono provides the sound track herself: mainly it is Yoko making high-pitched fly noises. The room is now empty save for a few others and me.

"In this film," says the guide, "Yoko is playing with our sense of space and sound. At points, it looks as if the fly is trying to climb a giant mountain."

"Bzzzzzzzzzzzzzzzzzzzzzzzzzz," says Yoko. "Eighneingengzzzzz!"

There is a ladder in the middle of the next exhibit room. "If you climb the ladder," says our guide, "you will see a magnifying glass and a tiny word. Thirty years ago, John Lennon climbed up and read that word, and he fell in love with the artist at that instant. Do you know what the word was?"

Nobody ventures a guess.

"I'll give you a hint . . . it's the name of the exhibit."

Nobody seems to remember the name of the exhibit.

"The word is *yes*. Yoko is very positive."

"A bunch of kooks," says the woman next to me. "They deserve each other."

Half of our group leaves early to go back to the bus and wait. The rest of the women shuffle on through the museum, but I stay behind and try to climb the ladder to read the word "Yes." Unfortunately, a security guard quickly yells out and disabuses me of that idea. Oh well. So much for the free-spirited sixties. It's too bad. I really wanted to know how John Lennon felt when he fell in love with Yoko. All that positivity. I've never really been a yes-type person. It's like this other Yoko exhibit in the museum, this maze. You wind your way around—it's harder than you expect—and when you reach the center, there's a toilet bowl. That's exactly my fear when I go out on a date. But then again, the guide says,

"Yoko intends her maze to mean different things to different people." Maybe to other people the toilet in the center of the maze symbolizes good things. Relief. Reality. Clarity. To me, it's just someone getting dumped. What have I missed out on? How great would it be to be in a relationship like John and Yoko's? To be able to sit around all day making a black-and-white film of my lover's genitals?

I wonder if Yoko would want to be my date to the wedding.

On the bus ride to lunch, everything begins to go to hell. Only a few of the women in the Art Appreciation Club seem to appreciate the art. The rest want their money back. It's one of those situations where what appeared at first to be a formless gray blob of old women turns out to be an intricate tapestry of divisions and subgroups. The wealthier women, who live on the east side of Boca, are claiming to have liked the exhibit. They are implying—no, they are out-and-out saying—that the women from the west side of Boca are classless and uncultured. The east siders want to stop at Ann Taylor before lunch, and the west siders get revenge by refusing to stop. "It's not on the itinerary!" they say. At lunch, a détente is reached when the food is terrible, and everyone temporarily joins forces to complain for an hour. The trip leader appears to be on the verge of tears.

"Who are your favorite artists?" I say, hoping to make peace.

"This chicken is too dry," they answer.

I'll say this: I don't know if Yoko Ono broke up the Beatles, but she definitely broke up my bus trip.

That night at the bingo hall, I notice that I am dangerously close to winning the Hatpin game. To win Hatpin, you need to get this pattern:

BINGO
39 7 66
4 10 23
79 21 SPACE 63 12
11 75 24 20
8 16 31 1

I have this:

BINGO
39 7 66
6 4 10 23
79 21 SPACE 63 12
11 75 24 20
8 16 31 1

As I move closer to my own bingo, box by box, I can feel excitement building in me: my heart beginning to beat faster, my palms sweating a little, a heightened awareness and thrumming inside my mind. I've noticed that when one of the women does win bingo, she shouts out the word with passion and disbelief. She has a big grin and flushed face. She savors the moment, her Brooklyn accent somehow wringing four or five syllables out of the word: "Ba-ying-gow-whoa!"

Yoko would love this place. It's living, breathing conceptual art. She would be inspired, I bet. She would say bingo is a symbolic tribute to the feminine relationship with winning. "The Deferred Orgasm," Yoko would call it. And Yoko would know how to take the concept over the top. Some kind of interactive piece where we all surround Yoko and dab her until her body is colored in ink, and then she starts shrieking, "Bingo! Bingo! Bingo! Yes! Yes! Yes!"

"Ba-ying-gow-whoa-whoo!" shouts a woman somewhere off in the distance.

"Man," I say. "I almost had that one."

"That's the way it goes," says Patty, the former teacher who got shot. She plays next to me most of the time now. "One of us wins, three hundred of us lose, try again next time."

"When's the last time you won?" I ask her.

She shrugs. "Couple months ago."

"How many times a week do you come here?"

"Couple times. Three or four times. But it's fun anyway."

After bingo, Patty and I walk out to the parking lot together. She has a favorite CD that she has been listening to recently, and she insists that we go over to her minivan to hear it. It is REO Speedwagon's greatest-hits album. "Sometimes I just put it on repeat and I just drive, vroooooom!" she says. She plays "Can't Fight This Feeling" for me as the parking lot empties.

After a minute, Patty climbs into the car and drives off onto

Atlantic Avenue, and I hear REO Speedwagon disappearing into the distance for quite some time. I feel like I'm back in junior high school, standing outside a Rec League dance. On a whim, I call my friend Jill in New York. Everyone always jokes about the fact that we should have dated.

"What the hell are you doing?" she says. "It's Saturday night."

"I went to a Yoko Ono art exhibit," I say, "and then I played bingo again."

"Jesus," she says. "Sweetie, you gotta get out of there."

"Do you want to go with me to my sister's wedding?" I say. Then, by way of extra enticement, I add: "It's not going to suck."

She says yes.

PLAYING PIANO

IT'S BEEN BOTHERING ME that Margaret never plays her piano. She doesn't appear to have many friends or social appointments. Though she and I have been talking more in recent weeks, we're not that close. Still, she talks more to me than to anyone else. I've been reading more books about aging, and it is quite clear that the more elderly retirees socialize, the longer they live and the happier they are. The alternative is not so good. In the United States, the highest rate of suicide is for those over age sixty-five, and has been since 1933, when they began keeping statistics.

I'm not sure what I'm supposed to do about Margaret. I go back and forth. Margaret isn't my family. Therefore, she isn't my problem. And I do pay most of her rent, so I am helping her anyway, regardless of my reluctance to get involved.

Yet it's hard to watch Margaret live her life and not feel some sense of duty. At those times, I want to give Margaret some tough love and shake her out of her funk. Here's what I would say, in the nicest way possible: What kind of way is it to live, alone, with no friends and horrible cats? It's been two years since your husband passed away. Couldn't you move on and get back out there? Join the Newcomers Club, or the Art Appreciation Club? Hang out with my pool group? I could help her get in with them. She knows me, and I have good connections there.

What else can I do to help Margaret?

To begin with, her progress has been impeded by the cats and parrots. She lives in constant fear that they will be taken away from her. That's a big reason she lives so privately and doesn't go out much.

"Make sure you close the door quickly when you leave, and keep the blinds and cat guard shut," she has said to me many times. "I don't want anyone to see the kitties."

Would it be the worst thing in the world if I somehow helped get rid of the animals? It would be horrible at first, but better for Margaret in the long run. I don't think I could ever kill the cats myself, but I could stuff them in a sack, climb the highest tree I can find, and leave them there. But I'm sure they'd somehow get down and come back more pissed than ever. It must mean something that you never see cat skeletons in trees.

Or I could "accidentally" leave the cat guard open and let the cats wander outside a bit near the waterways, so the neighbors could see them. Paula, the building gossip, told me that there have been complaints made to the building manager about Margaret's cats and birds. Maybe one more incident would galvanize him to action.

In fairness, Margaret is not totally helpless. I've learned that she has been trying for months to give piano lessons again. She has put several ads in the *Pennysaver* and heard nothing.

"Maybe nobody reads the *Pennysaver,*" she says.

"Yeah, maybe," I say, which is ridiculous. Everyone reads the *Pennysaver.*

"There aren't a lot of children around here," she says, "so there's not a lot of need for a piano teacher."

"I would do it," I say. "Would you want to teach me piano?" It seems like a reasonable favor to do for her. It might give her some confidence. Not to mention that it gets me in the habit of "actively working to keep the mind sharp," which I keep reading is important. But then I keep thinking about Amy Ballinger, and how squirmy she got when I asserted myself and tried to help her. If I should learn anything from this experience, it's that people, at the end of their life, ought to be able to do things how they want to. It's like this other study I read about in the MacArthur report that showed elderly people accomplish the most when they're encouraged to do things themselves, not when you do things for them: "We can only speculate on the frequency with which well-meaning or impatient younger people do things for their elders that they could do for themselves, and thus promote increasing helplessness and dependence. . . ."

"You want to learn piano?" Margaret says. The very idea of it is blowing her mind. I take a deep breath and make a fast decision.

"Sure," I say. "I always wanted to know how to play piano."

"Yes," she says. She seems pleased. "Very good. It's twenty dollars a lesson."

Which is a little surprising. I mean, you would think the woman could cut me a break on the fee—she's my *roommate.*

* * *

At my first piano lesson, the first thing we do is kick the cats off the piano. It takes them a moment to even realize what's going on. Nobody ever messes with them on the piano. Nobody ever raises their voice to them.

"Git!" says Margaret. "Go on, Ranchi! Git!"

They leap off the piano and stalk to the back of the condo. I had predicted this, and made sure that my bedroom door was closed, so as far as that goes, not to worry. I sit down on the left side of the piano bench. Margaret pulls up a dining room chair and sits next to the bench, way off to the right side of the keyboard.

"You can . . . you can sit on the bench with me if you want," I say.

"Oh . . . all right. Okay," Margaret says. She moves from the chair to the piano with an awkward lurch. I understand her trepidation; it feels strange to share a piece of furniture with someone whom you have been laboring to avoid for months.

We spend the first fifteen minutes going over a basic C scale. Margaret is quiet when we begin, but by a few scales in she's warming up as a teacher. It's a whole new side of her that I'm glad I'm getting to see. She has that classic music teacher persona that combines tenderness with menace. When I do things right she says, "Yes! Yes! Very good!" and when I screw up, she barks, "Not like that!"

"You're crossing the wrong finger over," Margaret says, when I mess up the scale's left-hand fingering. "Cross your middle finger over." She reaches over and touches my hand, tapping on my middle finger.

"Right," I say, "middle finger, middle finger, got it."

We do the C scale over and over again, and soon my middle-finger muscle memory kicks in, and I begin to sound okay. I no longer sound like an incredibly stupid six-year-old; I now sound like an eight-year-old of lower-than-average intelligence. It feels good.

"Do you smell something?" says Margaret.

I assume she is referring to the smell of me burning up the piano keys with my unalloyed talent. But she is in fact referring to the acrid odor that is beginning to fill the entire living room. We look around. It doesn't take long to discover the cat, sitting with pride next to an enormous pile of steaming cat feces.

"Ranchipurr!" she shouts, and he runs out of the room. "What a misbehaver!" she says, and she gets up and picks up the feces with a paper napkin, tossing it into the litter nearby.

"Well, that's it for today," says Margaret. I'm quite certain I would have gotten another five minutes if Ranchipurr hadn't interrupted. I, of course, understand the message that Ranchipurr was laying down, and the understanding strengthens my conviction that he has to go. We were making progress, and he doesn't want that to happen. That's my take on it. I know my friend Eva, who understands cats, would say that Ranchipurr was just upset that we were on his turf and using his bed to make an unbearable cacophony. Eva is wrong on this matter.

I pay Margaret the twenty dollars. I notice she doesn't have any other cash in her wallet. We continue to sit on the bench despite the lesson being over. She faces the piano and I face the other way.

"Do you ever think of getting rid of the cats and birds?" I say. "Give you a little less to take care of?" I'm hoping to take advantage of this moment and drive a wedge between her and the animals.

"Oh no!" says Margaret. "I love them. We're friends. Dan loved them too; we named them together."

"Dan, your husband?"

"Yes," she says, "my husband."

"How did he pass away?" I say, a risky gambit since Margaret never acknowledges that he's dead at all. I've been curious, though, how he died at a young age, in his mid-sixties.

Modern medicine tends to keep most people alive longer than that these days.

"We were down here in Florida looking for condos," says Margaret, "and we found this one. We both loved it and knew it was the one. We decided we would buy it. It was a very big decision for us. So we flew back North and went home, and we decided that very night to celebrate. I went out and bought a bottle of tequila, which was Dan's favorite. We both had a glass of tequila, and then he went inside to watch TV. A few hours later I went in to join him, and he was sleeping. I noticed that he had drunk the rest of the bottle of tequila. He had passed out. I didn't think anything of it. I went to bed. I woke up in the middle of the night and Dan was sleeping on the floor. I tried to wake him but he wouldn't get up. I called the doorman and he came up and he tried too. He said that Dan wasn't breathing, and he . . . he wasn't breathing and he . . . he didn't wake up," Margaret says.

She's fighting back tears now. Petna has walked back into the room and is watching me from the couch. I say nothing for a very long time, and then I say, "Wow . . . ," which is all I can think of. I put my hand on the back of her hand for a clumsy second, but it doesn't seem to be having any effect, so I stop.

"But you still moved down here," I say.

"Yes, we'd picked it out together," she says. "Just like this one here, Petna."

Petna jumps up and sits on top of the piano, staring at both of us now.

"Do you like cats?" says Margaret. Margaret pets Petna, and looks at me with some expectation. I reach my hand out toward the cat, and move it laterally on his fur for a few seconds.

"Yes, I do like cats," I say.

"Yes," says Margaret, "they're so independent and mysterious. That's why we love them."

"Exactly," I say.

I pull my hand away from Petna. Petna follows my palm and starts licking it with his scratchy tongue. "He likes you," says Margaret. I let him lick it for a while. It feels okay.

Later, I wash my hands approximately three thousand times.

ADORABLE

WARNING
A poem by Jenny Joseph

When I am an old woman I shall wear purple
With a red hat which doesn't go and doesn't suit me. . . .

AT NINE IN THE MORNING, the twenty Peppy Purple-ites of the Red Hat Society are gathering by the gangplank of the gambling cruise. Their advertising doesn't lie; they are very peppy. Red Hat Society rules dictate that you wear a red hat and a purple dress, but members are urged to bend the rules. There are bright purple dresses, light purple skirts, ambulance siren skirts, deep twilight skirts, grape jelly skirts, and a huge assortment of red caps, boaters, and brims. The women have also accessorized, somewhat insanely, with bright fake flowers, tiny stuffed birds glued to their hatbands, and jumbo earrings that hang off their heads like overripe grapes. Gathered together, the Peppy Purple-ites give the overall impression that owing to dwindling membership, a Nancy Reagan fan club and a Carmen Miranda fan club have decided to merge. That, or they are at a convention of the National Association for the Advancement of Chatty Older Ladies You Sometimes Meet at Bus Stops.

I was invited to join the Red Hat Society by Amy Ballinger, my ninety-three-year-old friend and former stand-up comedian. Several times a year, they take a trip on the *Princess of the Sea,* a four-tiered ship that travels for the day to international waters, where gambling is legal.

Instead of being her chauffeur, Amy explains, my function now is to be her arm candy. But within seconds of arriving, Amy abandons her candy and disappears to catch up with her fellow club members. I stand lost on the side until Amy takes pity on me and introduces me to Millie, the Queen Mother of the Peppy Purple-ites.

The first Red Hat Society, Millie explains, was founded in Fullerton, California, by Sue Ellen Cooper in the late 1990s. Though the club was intended for fifty-somethings hoping to smooth their passage into seniorhood, it has found its most enthusiastic participants in women who are already receiving Social Security checks. Within a few years of Sue Ellen Cooper's conception of the group, hundreds of chapters had sprung up, with the largest concentrations occurring in the retiree-heavy regions of Florida and Southern California. Each chapter has its own distinct alliterative name: the Crimson Chaos, the Hi-Steppin Hatters, or the chapter I'm with today, the Peppy Purple-ites of Palm Beach.

The mission statement of the Red Hat Society, as posted on their official website, is for women to greet their senior years "with humor, élan, and verve." Or, as Millie explains it, "with vim, vigor, and vitality." Basically, a lot of *V* words that sound like laundry detergents.

"We believe silliness is the comedy relief of life," explains Millie. "So every month, we gather in the name of acting silly."

"Tell him the truth," says Amy, laughing. "It's nothing but a bunch of lonely old goats."

The Peppy Purple-ites pull together and begin to board the boat, chattering and squealing. They're charging the saltwater air with their excitement, drowning out seagulls. We talk over one another about what games we're going to play on board, about the damage we'll be doing at the buffet. The gamblers around us, heavy-lidded and male, have no clue what to make of the women. One of them gasps, "Holy shit!" as the Purple-ites storm by.

We come to a halt at the security checkpoint. Almost a third of the Red Hatters have neglected to bring picture ID, a strictly enforced requirement of anyone boarding the gambling ship.

"If we were supposed to bring ID, you should have told us in advance!" one of the women complains.

The low-level security guards confer, unsure of what to do. It would be embarrassing for them if this gaggle of giggling old women turned out to be terrorists, some kind of brilliant al-Qaeda Trojan horse where, once inside, the purple dress seams would split open, revealing gun-toting Saudis.

"We're the Red Hatters!" complains Millie to the nearest guard.

"I'm sorry, ma'am, I really am. Our supervisor is on his way," the guard says, fidgeting.

"Why don't you just let them through," I say. "They're just trying to have a good time." He stares at me. Amy steps up to my side to try a different approach. She points at my two-day beard growth, and shouts to the guard, "Why are you stopping us? He's the one who looks like a terrorist."

That works only in the sense that it earns me a trip to the overstaffed side table, where three security guards take particular interest in the baffling mechanisms of my miniature tape recorder.

Hector, the supervisor, arrives, and looks at the Peppy Purple-ites stone-faced for a good ten seconds. "You ladies are the most adorable thing I've ever seen," he says. The women begin to blush from the pleasure of the compliment. Hector tells his underlings to let everyone on.

Well, not everyone. I'm detained another five minutes so they can check my laptop computer for explosives. Apparently I'm not adorable enough.

Adorable is a word you encounter a lot when you're spending time with older people. It's one of the only ways we compliment older people on their physical appearance, as in: "Isn't that little old lady adorable?" or "Look at that old man lifting weights. He's adorable!" That's what my television agent said the other day on the phone, when I told her I was hanging out with the Red Hatters. "They sound adorable." Then my agent asked me if I planned on coming home to start working again anytime soon, and I more or less pretended there was cell phone interference in Florida, the flattest state in the country.

Old women aren't always considered adorable. Sometimes, if an older woman is lucky, she will be considered "handsome" or, if she's rich enough, "elegant." But somewhere in our sixties, the rest of us become adorable, like a baby or a puppy. Perhaps, as we age, our rounded, drooping, indistinct features are reminiscent of babies'. Perhaps the way our breathing grows labored and wet is reminiscent of puppies.

What does it feel like to be called "adorable" when at one time you were just "beautiful"? It's a loaded word, full of both admiration and pity. Adorable things are harmless things, unthreatening, but celebrated anyway. It's a devil's bargain. When the Peppy Purple-ites put on their purple dresses and red hats, they agree to be adorable.

Red sky at night, sailor's delight.
Red sky at morning, sailors take warning.

—Old sailors' saying

After we board the boat, I brace myself for serious silliness, vim, and vigor. But the women are pooped from the excitement at the gate, so they sit down in the lounge area and begin their monthly meeting. Within minutes, I'm bored out of my mind. It's like I'd imagine a church meeting to be, but we don't even have leftover bake sale brownies to eat for a sugar spike.

Patty, the Red Hatters' secretary, reads the minutes from the previous meeting. What makes it postmodern is the fact that the Red Hatters spent the previous meeting talking mainly about their upcoming trip on a gambling boat.

"The Red Hatters will be meeting at nine A.M. in the parking lot," reads Patty. "The *Princess of the Sea* boat has many amenities such as music entertainment, a variety of gambling attractions, and a large sitting area for our monthly meeting." Patty pauses to motion to the large sitting area we are currently meeting in, then continues. "Members were reminded to bring picture ID on the cruise or they will not be allowed aboard the boat."

I'm the only one paying any attention. Everyone else has glazed over. Amy Ballinger, sitting next to me, is napping outright. The only real excitement is watching the other boat passengers take in the purple. My guess is that they're hoping that where there are elderly women in funny outfits, there must be a *Today* show camera crew.

A portly tourist separates from her husband and approaches the women.

"Okay, I just have to ask," she says. "What's with the red hats?"

Millie perks herself up in her chair. "They mean we're ladies of the Red Hat Society, full of vim and vigor," she says.

"Oh, I heard of this," says the woman. "It's like one of those clubs you join when your husband dies?"

"No," says Millie, offended. "Not at all. Any woman over fifty can join. Would you like to join?"

"Nah, I still got a fella hanging around," says the woman. "Not for me."

A one-man band on a Casiotone is playing "Kokomo" in the corner, singing off-key about getting there fast and taking it slow. Everyone sits. We're taking it very slow right now. Millie, trying to buoy the Red Hatters' mood, claps her hands together. "Ladies! Ladies! Did I *tell* you? Did I tell you I spoke for nearly *fifteen minutes* on the telephone to the *EQM*?"

Ah yes. The EQM. Now would be a good time to mention that the Red Hat Society is something of a cult. It's not a cult-cult. It's not a Scientology cult. Members aren't expected to make monetary donations to the society, or take expensive classes so they can achieve higher levels of "redness." It is a cult more like organized religions are cults. When Sue Ellen Cooper invented her doctrine of silliness, she became an unknowable deity to hundreds of elderly Florida women. They call her the Exalted Queen Mother, or sometimes the EQM. They speak of her in hushed tones; she rules over the Red Armies from a far-off land called Orange County.

"The EQM is very pleased that our club is doing so well," says Millie. "She sends her regards to everyone and invites us to stop in and visit if we're ever in the area." Her story has the desired effect. Proximity to the EQM delights the Red Hatters. Their smiles widen and their spines lengthen as they bask in the sunlight of the Exalted Queen Mother.

"That's wonderful of her to say that," says a Red Hatter. "She didn't have to."

"But she *did*!" says Millie. She beams at everyone and soon they're beaming back. The boat has left the dock and is steaming into international waters. "Who's ready for gambling?" asks Millie.

The Red Hatters let out a loud cheer, which grows louder still as they're energized by the spectacle they're making. The one-man band stops the "Kokomo" as he realizes he's outmatched. I wish I'd brought my roommate, Margaret, along with me; she would have kicked this clown right off the keyboards.

In the casino room, fifty slot machines sit side by side. They have names like "Instant Winner," "Filthy Rich!" and "Boom!" I don't hear much money being won, but the machines do belch an endless arrhythmic calliope of bells and dings. Clutching plastic cups full of coins, the Red Hatters face the slots. Old women seem to love slot machines.

I've been demoted to a sort of coin caddy, toting the plastic cups of coins around for Amy and some other women. It's demeaning, perhaps, but not as emasculating as carrying a purse. The women are rapt. They hit the spin button, *tap, tap, tap, tap, tap,* as their losses pile up.

"This is daylight robbery," Amy keeps saying, and then tells me to go get her change for a twenty.

What would the EQM, Sue Ellen Cooper, do if she could see us now? Would she be enraged? Would she descend from the clouds on crimson horseback, throwing purple thunderbolts at her wayward daughters? Gambling on a boat isn't exactly running in the rain, like the poem urges us to do. We're not exactly stealing flowers. In fact, the only things that seem to be getting stolen here are Social Security checks. "It's daylight robbery in here," mutters Amy Ballinger again, grabbing more coins out of the cup. I'm pretty sure it's my money she's betting now. I feel compelled to tear these women away from the machines, staging a Red Hat intervention. We should be leapfrogging up on the wet deck, or in a dinghy teaching manatees dirty limericks. We should be grabbing control of the wheel and going full speed, steering daffodil designs on top of the whitecaps. We are Red Hatters!

And then, a manic mix of sudden shouting sings out from some Peppy Purple-ites. Minnie has won $1,500 on a two-quarter slot machine.

The Peppy Purple-ites are drinking. Minnie has been buying rounds for the last hour from a Filipino bartender who tosses bottles like Tom Cruise in *Cocktail*. I've had four vodka cranberries, which is the drink you get when you leave your drink choice up to an eighty-five-year-old woman.

The Peppy Purple-ites are disco dancing. Specifically, they are disco line dancing. They move in unison, stomping and clapping, as the one-man band plays "Dancing Queen." The EQM would approve. If she were here she would be quite drunk, dancing to the synthesized beats and pointing at herself whenever the singer says "queen."

Amy Ballinger and I sit at the bar. Amy's ninety-three-year-old knees are bothering her, but she wouldn't want to be up there anyway. We comedians don't line dance.

"I knew somebody would win," says Amy.

"I didn't," I say, but I'm glad that somebody did. Luck has unleashed them more than I could have imagined. The one-man band is playing a tarantella now, faster and faster, his hands jabbing the keys in escalating vamps. Some red hats have been tossed off. The women are shifting and spinning with demonic ferocity. Their wispy, dark gray hair flies up, their red dresses rustle, and I am blushing now. They look strange and unmistakably sexy, like young witches dancing around a campfire. The male gamblers have gathered at the sides of the dance floor and are staring. Some try to dance with the women, but they crap out. They can't keep up.

"They look adorable," I say. The words just slip out.

"No, they don't," says Amy. "They look like sex on shoes."

The women come to get me and pull me onto the dance floor. At some point, I may have been wearing a red hat. Later on, I remember Amy boozily teaching me a toast: "When the night is hot and sultry, that is not the time for adultery. But when the frost is on the pumpkin, that is the time for peter dunkin'."

The music stops, the boat docks, and the money is collected from the machines. The ladies say good-bye. That evening, dresses are hung in the closet next to cotton-poly slacks. The Purple-ites go back to bridge and aquafit, their old-lady things, until next month, when, if luck is with them, the peppy purple-wearing widows will gather and dance again.

THE GREATEST GENERATION

MOST OF THE MALE SENIOR CITIZENS I meet in Florida are World War II veterans. It's humbling to talk to them about those years. I hear a lot of heroic stories, the kind that have already filled numerous books written by television news anchors.

What we haven't heard, though, are the WWII stories that are dull or uneventful. Because, let me tell you, many WWII stories are. Many of the men I spoke with didn't storm Normandy or Iwo Jima. They will never be played by Tom Hanks or the Duke. One man, for instance, was sent to Germany several months after V-E Day. He says that he "sat on his ass for two years, and did a lot of drinking and chasing German women. It was like a vacation." Another man was a typist in the U.S. Army. Stationed in Atlanta. "It wasn't so bad," he said.

If there is a publisher out there that wants to fund a compilation of these stories, I will serve as editor so these voices can be heard. Until then, I give you the story of Leon, in his own words:

> "I was stationed in Basra, in the south of Iraq. I served in the Royal Air Force of England. I was there for two years, but I have very little recollection. Almost none. Not much happened. We were five thousand miles from the nearest theater of war. This was years before there was any reason for an army to be in Iraq.
>
> "I didn't see any enemy soldiers when I was there. Not one. I couldn't even tell you what a German looked like, what a German flag looked like. We did see one Russian soldier, once. We were eating in the dining room and he walked through. He didn't have a gun.
>
> "I didn't carry a gun. I had no weapons, no, none. Didn't carry one. I had weapons training, of course. I once flew a grenade over the fence. Target shooting. But that's about all. After that I didn't see any weapons.
>
> "Why were we there? That's a good question. Well, we were there to get rid of the bombs. Thirty-pound bombs, stacked in huts. We did that every day, all day long. I don't remember why. They were left over from World War I. The Arabs, nomads, we called them, they would put them on the truck, and we took them to the railroad sidings, and the Sikhs would load them onto a train. I don't recall where they went after that. I didn't ever ask, I don't think.
>
> "What did we do? We lay in our beds, our bunks, listening to our radios. We ate local food, pita bread, dates, and cheese. We ate Spam. There was no such thing as Coca-Cola there then, to my knowledge. But there was ice cream. I remember that. We had peanuts

and chestnuts, too. They were very popular. We ate a lot.

"I didn't date women when I was in Iraq. Only one man in our barracks had an Iraqi girlfriend. A handsome-looking man. There were legalized brothels in Iraq. I visited one out of curiosity. I just wanted to see the inside. It had nothing to do with the women. I just sat on the couch as the other men went inside with the women. They came out and we went home.

"That was more or less it. Two years. My duty was just dodging mosquitoes more than anything. Yes, mosquitoes, that was the worst of it; we had to sleep in nets, they were so bad.

"I was never bit, though. Not to my recollection."

C.O.P.S

Marvin is ninety years old. He's got terrible hearing. He goes to his annual physical with his wife. His doctor says, "Marvin, I'm going to need a stool sample, a urine sample, and a semen sample." Marvin can't hear him—he says: "What did you say?" The doctor says, "I'm gonna need a stool sample, a urine sample, and a semen sample!" Marvin says, "WHAT DID YOU SAY?" Finally his wife looks at him and says, "He wants you to give him your pants, Marvin!"

—Joke told to me by Amy Ballinger

I AM DRIVING ON THE INTERCOASTAL HIGHWAY when my peripheral vision tells me that a police officer has pulled alongside me. I freak out, as I always do when I see a police car. The fear of police is so gut level it must be primal. Take a look in your rearview mirror next time you pass a cop and watch people react. If I were a cop, I would get off on it; just sitting on the side of the road watching the brake lights flash as people freak out.

The cop drives next to me, matching my speed. I focus on the road and pretend not to notice him. Finally, as we are both stopped at a red light, I sneak a look. And there, driving the regulation police car is a ninety-five-year-old man in a police uniform.

After a few months in Florida I've seen enough elderly cops that I have developed a curiosity. I ask around, and I am directed to the office of Lieutenant Jeffrey Lindskoog of the Palm Beach Sheriff's Department. The sheriff's department is located in an outdoor shopping center next to a Winn Dixie supermarket. From the outside, it pretty much looks like a Mail Boxes Etc.

Lindskoog himself is a watchful, serious man with a serious, watchful mustache. He gives off the impression that no matter what I could say to him, I would be wasting his time. Lindskoog explains to me that the "elderly cops"—he uses my phrase with obvious disdain—are members of the Palm Beach Sheriff's Department's C.O.P. unit. Their official name is the Citizens Observer Patrol. C.O.P. is an unpaid division, with over 5,500 volunteers. It is the largest volunteer crime prevention program in the United States, and the majority of volunteers are retirees over the age of sixty-five.

"The volunteers," Lieutenant Lindskoog makes very clear, "have no authority to make arrests." They are the "eyes and ears" of the police department. Their job is to patrol the areas around where they live and alert the sheriff's department if they see anything unusual or illegal. The C.O.P. program has a total of 125 police cars, which are supplied and maintained by the sheriff's department. Each C.O.P. vehicle is equipped with a cellular phone and police scanner. "Why did you guys decide to have a program like this?" I ask. I'm hoping that Lindskoog understands the implicit question underneath it, which is "Why would you willingly put more elderly drivers on the road?"

"The C.O.P. program saves the department millions of dollars a year," Lindskoog tells me. By increasing police visibility, the volunteers act as a crime deterrent. They also take care of a lot of the sheriff's department's non–law enforcement responsibilities: fingerprinting, safety demonstrations, record keeping, and clerical work. Not to mention, Lindskoog adds, "They give generously to the Policeman's Benevolent Association because they really feel like they're a part of the department."

I continue to ask Lindskoog questions, and my interest gradually seems to soften him, except for when I ask him if they've ever considered letting elderly people run a volunteer ambulance program, and he looks at me like I'm a moron. At the end of our meeting he offers to arrange for me to spend a day or two doing a "ride-along" with one of the volunteers.

"Ride along?" I say. "You mean, like, on their patrol?"

"Yes," he says.

"Will I get to wear a uniform?" I say, doing a bad job of masking my excitement.

"Absolutely not," he says.

"Very good, then," I say. "Sounds good."

I'm not surprised that so many retired men want to be police officers. It's hard to be a retired man. Think about it: the transition from working man can be brutal. Once men leave their jobs, they are losing the thing that defined them for most of their adult life. The thing that was on their business card, right under their name. Forty years of breadwinning are over; they have no power. Furthermore, they have nothing to do all day. *Successful Aging* says that "leaving their job deprives [men] of a major source of stimulation. They need to find it in other ways."

After they retire, it seems that the first way many men seek stimulation is by accompanying their wives on shopping expeditions. I've seen loads of recent male retirees sitting on benches outside department stores, waiting for their wives to finish trying on blouses. Shirley from the Pool Group has names for these sorts of men. She calls them the "Wife's Best Friend," or the "Mensch on the Bench." I always feel sorry for those guys when I see them. They look like they've been swimming in cold water for months.

Once a man lives like this for a while he's bound to want to fight back. For this reason, I am looking forward to my C.O.P. ride-along. The way I see it, if you give a man like this a police uniform and some authority, the stage is set for him to snap in a spectacular fashion. I want to be there when that happens. That's the kind of excitement I'm craving after a few months of boat trips and bus rides with elderly women. Around Century Village I had already begun to hear stories about how some of these C.O.P.s have difficulty with the "eyes and ears" aspect of their job, and sometimes add "mouth" and "fists." Last Halloween, some kids threw eggs at an in-uniform C.O.P. member, and the member decided to engage in a high-speed car chase in excess of 100 miles per hour, all the while cursing up a storm out his window. I'd asked Lindskoog about it, and he'd denied it, so it's probably true. I'd heard about the policeman's code, the "blue wall" of silence.

I have been assigned to a C.O.P. officer named Steven Goldman. At first I interpret this as slight anti-Semitism. Put the Jew with a Jew. That was before I knew that most of the C.O.P. volunteers are Jewish. Within five minutes of arriving at the C.O.P. substation, I have met a former shoe salesman named Murray, a former schoolteacher named Natalie, and a former bra salesman named Mel who proclaims himself "king of the boobs." All are over seventy-five years old and are uniformed C.O.P.s. We sit in the office and drink morning coffee, and there's no sense that anyone will be rushing off anytime soon. I ask if anything exciting has happened recently, and I am told that they fingerprinted over five hundred schoolchildren last week, and that several years ago a volunteer saved someone from choking at an all-you-can-eat buffet.

Lieutenant Steven Goldman is a large, jovial man. Yes, he

has a mustache, but it's a laid-back one; it's like a fluffy white sheepdog napping on his face. Goldman is the kind of guy who seems to be able to converse with anybody about anything. He seems like the kind of cop who, if he were shot in the line of duty, would still find a way to say his assailant is "a good guy."

"What did you used to do?" I say.

"I'm a former government agent," he says.

"Wow," I say, "that sounds important. What kind?"

"I was a grain industry compliance officer."

"Oh," I say. "That was important?"

"You bet," he says. "Kept organized crime out of the grain business for twenty years."

I've got my doubts, but my hope is that Goldman is a prime candidate to lose his C.O.P. temper. He seems so nice. How could he not have all kinds of rage bottled up within? One indication that he does: he and another man in the substation, Lieutenant Muros, refer to regular and decaf coffee as "leaded and unleaded." Classic tough-guy move.

Goldman and I hop in our cop car and begin to drive around the area. I've never been in an actual moving police car before.

We've been driving for a few seconds, and I already have a pretty uncontrollable desire to play cops and robbers. Why did I assume that only old men would feel this urge? The first thing I think we should do is kick our car up above the speed limit. Though our cop car is a Lumina, I've heard about how cops deck out their seemingly unimpressive sedans. That's what allows them to blaze by you on the highway in that signature dick-cop move, the "I can speed and you can't" maneuver.

"I bet this thing can move," I say to Goldman. I give him an eyebrow bounce, indicating: Come on, man. Let's show off.

"Unfortunately, no, it can't move," he says. "It can't get out of its own way. They give the cars to us when they're kaput."

"Oh," I say, because that doesn't feel very powerful at all, to be fighting crime in a rental car.

I've been watching the TV show *COPS* for years. It makes police work seem thrilling. Even on a slow day on *COPS,* they're running, jumping, yelling, calling for backup. They're busting prostitutes, car thieves, deadbeat dads. And fifteen times an hour, they're chasing drunk drivers until they barrel into garbage cans. It's good stuff.

If you made a TV show about Goldman and the C.O.P.s, though, you'd be in for a somewhat Buddhist riff on the genre. The C.O.P.s drive in aimless circles, for hours on end. They don't run, chase, or radio. They bust nobody. Every once in a while they pull in to shopping centers to "look for anything unusual." So far the most unusual thing Goldman has pointed out is some "joker" who parked his Camry so that it took up two spaces instead of one.

I'll say this, though: Goldman takes this partner thing seriously. He acts like we've been in the same car for decades. He talks a lot, but not like I'd want my cop partner to talk. Rather than talk about sports or marital infidelity, he is more likely to say things like: "Check those clouds out, they're something, huh?" or "You should go to Paris, Paris is lovely." Goldman and his wife were there last year, and though he just met me, he claims that he knows the perfect girl for me, a Moroccan Jew working as a waitress in Pigalle. Are cop partners supposed to set each other up with nice Jewish girls?

"Maybe you haven't met the right girl yet," he says to me, and I think: Dude, cops aren't supposed to say that either.

Our conversation meanders, changing topics several times a minute. The talking and the driving remind me of being a stoned teenager with no party to go to. The weird thing is, when I was a stoned teenager, the main thing we were scared of was a cop. And the cops were everywhere back then. So where the hell are the stoned teenagers now?

There is a natural polarity to police partners. That's obvious to any fan of the genre. If one partner is nice, that means the other partner is a bastard. If one is old and worn out, the other is young and energetic. If one is a "loose cannon," the other is a "team player." I feel these forces at play as I ride around with Goldman. Goldman is a goody-goody. It's pretty clear to me now that Lindskoog set me up with his model cop on purpose. He doesn't want any bad press. Goldman even claims that he never accepted a bribe in three decades of working against mobsters. That's hard to believe. Over the last few months in Florida, I've met a lot of retired policemen who openly admit they took bribes. According to one guy I know, Mo, the only way a cop could make a living back in the 1950s was by taking bribes. I once asked Mo why he became a cop, and he told me it was because of the corruption. It took me a few seconds to realize that he didn't mean fighting corruption; he meant getting a piece of it. "In order to survive," Mo says, "you have to have a certain amount of larceny in your life."

But that's not Goldman. I believe he never took a bribe. Goldman is good. And because Goldman is good, the law of police partners dictates that I must be bad. I must be bad cop. So while Goldman steers, I busy myself by glaring out the window at other drivers, trying to scare the bejesus out of them. The problem with that, which I should have guessed from my own experience, is that nobody looks at cops when they ride alongside them.

"It's kind of quiet out there," I say to Goldman.

"Yeah, you got that right," he says. He thinks I meant it in a good way.

"When are we gonna see some action?" I say, out loud, with no sense of how ridiculous I sound.

"Action!" says Goldman. Then he laughs and keeps driving. I'm confused. Was that his whole answer?

"Two Jews in a cop car," I say. "What are the odds of that?"

"What do you mean?" he says. "There are a lot of Jewish C.O.P.s."

"I know," I say, "but not, like, real cops."

"Sure there are," he says. "Did you know that thousands of Jews fought in the Civil War? In the Union and the Confederacy, did you know that?"

"Yeah?" I say, with some bitterness. "Are you sure it wasn't the C.O.N.federacy?"

Goldman laughs. "You want to get some lunch?" he asks me.

Goldman eats fast and sloppy, like I imagine a real cop would. Maybe, I think, Goldman does have a wild man within. Maybe he has a dark past. I know about the "blue wall." In C.O.P.s, I suppose it would be the "gray wall." Is Goldman hiding behind a gray wall?

"Hey, Steven," I say, "have you ever beaten anybody up on the job?"

"Oh God, no," says Goldman.

"You ever broken the law?"

"Nope." Goldman shrugs. "Well," he says, "a long time ago. When I was a kid. I stole some candy from a store. My father made me bring it back."

"Oh."

"What about you?" he asks.

"Me?" I hadn't expected him to turn the question around. My face is starting to turn a little red. "Yeah, I have," I say, and then I try to give a little bad-cop shrug.

"What for?" he says.

I chew, regretting this entire conversation.

"Nothing, really," I say.

"Ooooh," he says. "Sounds good!"

The thing is, Goldman has access to police computers. He could just look me up and find out.

"It's for, uh . . . it's for public urination," I say.

Goldman starts to laugh. "You got a pissing ticket?"

"Yeah," I say. "In Chinatown. In the rain." To be technical, it was a pissing summons, but I don't correct him. Does the Chinatown part make it seem less embarrassing? My guess is no. I got a public-pissing summons in a neighborhood where they routinely dump gecko blood onto the street. What kind of bad cop is told, as I was, via police loudspeaker, "You over there. Put your dick back in your pants and approach the car."?

We try to pay for the meal, but the waitress won't let us. I expect Goldman to insist, but he doesn't.

"Thanks for patrolling the neighborhood," she says.

"It's no problem," says Goldman. I look at him. Suddenly I understand that this little moment is the one he lives for. This is the larceny in his life; yes, even Goldman has to get his strut on.

This morning, for the first time in over a month, I spoke to some of my friends and family back home. I hadn't realized so much time had passed. My mom and dad had gone to the Berkshires for a week. My friend Dan in New York managed to squeeze in an entire relationship with a new girlfriend since we last spoke. My friend Eva not only decided to leave her job, but also observed the three-week notice and left it. Hearing all the news gave me mixed sensations, like I had missed out on things, but at the same time not quite caring because the news was the same old, same old, and nothing really had changed.

* * *

I am feeling distracted as we do our patrol. It's raining, and it's hard to make the road out, let alone locate suspicious characters. It has to be the sixtieth straight day of rain in the Sunshine State. Our conversation fits the weather and is more muted than usual. We've added some houses of worship to our patrol route, because the 9/11 anniversary is coming up. As we pass through a synagogue parking lot, Goldman tells me he is Jewish but believes in praying in any place of worship he can, since you never know which religion is the right one. That seems very Goldman to me; he's such a goody-goody he's afraid to offend any deity.

A few days later, I stop by the station looking for Goldman.

"He's not here," says Natalie, the retired schoolteacher C.O.P., as she puts on her raincoat. "He had to go. There was a bomb scare at Palmetto and Lyons. The bomb squad is there now with the canines, and they want us to put hazard lights up and control traffic." She's heading over there now.

For a moment, I am furious. There's a bomb scare and Goldman left without me? There's finally some action, and I've missed it by ten minutes because my so-called partner abandoned me? Then the fury mutates into confusion. Goldman is at a bomb scare? That seems insane. C.O.P.s shouldn't do things like that. We drive in circles, eat and talk about clouds; we don't go to bomb scares.

"Should I head over there in my rental car?" I ask Natalie. She moves across the room toward the door, appearing not to have heard me. My heart is beating fast. For all my talk about action, now I am beginning to recall that I hate actual action. "Are they okay?" I ask.

"I hope I don't need to get out of my car in the rain," says Natalie, her voice pinched. "All I need is frizz 'fro."

She walks out the door, leaving me alone. She gets in her car and drives off. Large sheets of grayish rain are falling outside. I notice my fists are a little balled up. Why didn't it ever occur to me to bring a raincoat or umbrella to Florida? Where did I get the idea it never rained here?

Not long after, Goldman bursts through the door.

"There you are," he says.

"What happened?"

"They sent us back," he says. "They had it covered."

Goldman makes a "phew" gesture, and heads into the back room. My body slackens with relief. Then, for a moment, I allow myself to feel righteous and angry again, because how often do you get a chance to run out in the rain to a bomb scene and be a hero, and if they had given us a shot, I bet Goldman and I could have been good at it.

We spend the rest of the afternoon sitting around the substation drinking unleaded. Above Goldman's desk is a sign: IT'S NICE TO BE IMPORTANT BUT IT'S MORE IMPORTANT TO BE NICE. Mel, the former bra salesman, points at it and tells me with a Marx Brothers accent: "That should say it's nice to be important, but it's more *impotent* to be nice."

Later, Natalie shows up. It turns out that the bomb was actually a wet paper lunch bag stuffed between the guardrail and a stone wall.

"I got frizz 'fro anyway," she says.

HOUSE HUNTING

I'VE DECIDED TO GO SHOPPING for my potential retirement home now, while I'm down here in Florida. I've made arrangements to visit some fifteen "active adult retirement communities" over the next week. As long as I'm here, it seems like a good use of my time. By the end of it I'll have homed in and given some real thought to what I may want later in life. I'm pretty sure I wouldn't want to live somewhere like Century Village. I probably wouldn't want other people on top of me quite so much, though in some ways, it's not that bad.

I'm not actually planning on buying a place now, although the notion has crossed my mind. It would be a great relief to just decide now how I would want to retire and get the whole issue out of the way. Not to mention that it could turn out to be an incredible investment. I met a woman at dinner the other night who lives by the Atlantic Ocean in a house.

"I bought my house twenty years ago for $40,000," one woman told me recently, "and it's worth ten times as much now." It's a tempting prospect. If I was able to buy my retirement home now, it could end up being the greatest investment of my life.

My first stop is a newly built community located on Jog Road. It's a few miles to the north of where I've been living, so I am already familiar with the neighborhood. That's a plus. The community consists of simple two-story buildings huddled around small man-made lakes—more than anything, it resembles a junior college.

As I start to meet with Mary, the sales agent, I'm faced for the first time with an intriguing challenge: How do you shop for a retirement community forty years early without creeping people out? Getting in the door isn't a factor; as I've learned, some active adult communities are required by antidiscrimination laws to have at least 20 percent of their residents be under their suggested minimum age.

You're the buyer, I remind myself, steeling my nerves. *You're in control. But don't be disagreeable. Don't forget that the seller isn't just selling, she's also buying a buyer.*

My solution is to work my situation with as much subtlety as possible. When Mary asks me what I'm doing there, I tell her, "I'm just checking out homes for the future. Maybe for my parents." Mary relaxes and smiles when I say that. Then I add: "Or maybe for my own retirement, thirty or forty years from now. It's more likely for that. Things are still up in the air." Mary hesitates. "We're looking to rent these units in the next few weeks," she says. "Yeah, yeah," I say. "That's when I'm looking for. Something in the next few weeks, or in the event things don't work out right now, for thirty years from now. For my retirement." Mary gets up to start showing me around.

"Well," she jokes, "I hope I'm not going to be working here then."

The stench of fresh carpeting is overpowering as we breeze through a few open units. "Note the beauty area," she says, stopping by a large vanity. "Are you married?" she asks. "Not right now," I say. "But I might be by the time I retire, so a beauty area could come in handy." Mary, at this point, is on sales overdrive, listening to nothing I'm saying. "All the fixtures are new," says Mary, fingering the bronze kitchen cabinet handles.

"They're nice," I say. "But how do you think this place will age? Do they have plans to renovate it later on?"

"Well," she says, "I guess they'd have to. You know . . . supply and demand."

We smile blankly at each other for an awkward moment. I figure I'm starting to cross into creepy, but she might not be convinced yet, since I'm wearing khakis, which are not creepy-person pants. I may have time for a few more pertinent questions.

"What about athletic facilities?" Mary, happy to be back on a topic she can recite from memory, says, "Certainly. We have tennis courts, a swimming pool. There's a fitness center in the main clubhouse."

"Okay," I say. "Let's say that sometime in the future there's some kind of new sport invented. Do you think that the athletic facilities would be expanded to accommodate that?"

"What do you mean, 'new sport'?" she says.

"Well, I don't even know, you know, it hasn't been invented yet. You know, something like jetpack soccer, but not that—that's just a bad example. We can't conceive of it yet, is my point."

"Well," says Mary, after seeming to consider my question. "That would be up to what the residents want. We're very reactive."

"Very good," I say.

Once you've visited five or six retirement communities in one day, it becomes very difficult to tell them apart from one another. Over and over again, you find yourself driving down a street called Everglade Lane, past nearly identical two-bedroom houses with attached garages and eight-foot-by-eight-foot sodded front yards. Sometimes the clubhouse has four tennis courts, sometimes it has five. Sometimes the sixty-year-old woman with dyed wheat-colored hair at the information desk is named Phyllis, other times she's named Francine. At some point someone will hand you a brochure featuring a full-page photo spread of robust elderly homeowners slow-dancing in South Florida moonlight. The community names start to blur too: Verona Lakes, Venetian Isles, Harbor Isles, Harborview, Fountainview, Lakeview. I'm concerned that when I pick the community I want to retire into, I'll have forgotten the name of it by the time I retire. I'll wander aimless and homeless around South Florida until I'm attacked and eaten by a displaced alligator.

The most generic community by far has to be Vizcaya, which I trudge into late on my first day of looking. Vizcaya is redundant on virtually every possible level. Vizcaya's houses are all painted an identical sand color, with virtually no stylistic variance—there's something Socialist about it. It feels like a retirement commune. I know that the name Vizcaya is supposed to evoke the feeling of Spanish gentility, but it sounds more like something Vladimir Putin would shout before downing a glass of vodka.

Why would I want to live in a place like this? Vizcaya makes me not want to retire because it forces me to associate retirement with letting go of everything that I consider unique about myself. I'm not an iconoclast, but I try to be distinctive. I might own a few Banana Republic pocket tees, but they tend to be in unexpected, less popular colors like hunter green. But what's the point of spending my entire life trying to be bigger, better, different from everyone else if I'm just going to cash it all in for the same stuff everyone else has? It's insulting. I'd rather be a crazy, unshaven old guy baking in an Airstream trailer on the edge of a desert, or one of those guys who balloons around the world and plummets uniquely and memorably into a little-known inland sea.

Soon after arriving, I'm interrogating a wheat-haired woman with an embroidered pony on her T-shirt at the information desk.

"Let's say I want to paint my house a different color, make it distinctive in some way. Would that be allowed in Vizcaya?"

"No. It's uniform. It would bring the neighborhood down."

She refers me to the list of house designs I picked up in the sales office, and I look it over. The houses look pretty much the same. I see the Andalusia, the Alcazar, and the Catalonia, meaningless Spanish names. Do they even have Spanish people living here, or would that bring the neighborhood down?

"These houses kind of look the same," I say.

"They're very similar."

"Is there a difference between the Andalusia and the Alcazar?"

"I think the Alcazar might be bigger."

"Much bigger?"

"No. Slightly bigger."

"Okay . . . I'm sorry to ask such a weird question, but are there any Spaniards living in Vizcaya?"

"I don't think so. We have Canadians."

"Thank you."

At the swimming pool one day, I ask the Pool Group about

their own retirement choices. Why come to Century Village, a somewhat bare-bones Boca Raton retirement community, every year when they could buy an RV and see the country, or at least go to the Gulf coast?

"That might be fun," says Shirley, "but our friends are here. We go where our friends go." I'm not one for lecturing my fellow Pool Group–ers on the soullessness of conformity, and I also understand what she's saying. It's comforting to go where your friends are. When I'm seventy-nine, am I going to want to be sleeping in a hostel, sharing a bunk bed with a German trance DJ for the sake of being different? Or will I be content sleeping in my Alcazar, knowing that it's a little bigger than my neighbor's Andalusia, knowing that I'm less than half a mile from a Canadian if I'm ever feeling adventurous?

The next morning, I decide to try the opposite extreme. Mizner Country Club is a luxurious community where the average house price is north of $1 million. But money doesn't just buy you a huge house with poured concrete Roman pillars by the swimming pool. It buys you distinction from the conformist masses. At Mizner, houses don't have "entrances," they have "great rooms." At Mizner, there's no clubhouse, but there is a "Grande Clubhouse." The implicit message is that Mizner will spare no expense—they're willing to incur the cost of adding an *e* to the word "Grand," so that you know you've got the "lifestyle you deserve." Mizner has forgone the typical Spanish-influenced names for their house styles, and gone with names that reek of moneyed opulence: "The Carrington," "The Aristocrat," "The Ambassador," which all sound like condoms to me.

When I told the Pool Group I was visiting Mizner, they let out an impressed "Wow," but with an undercurrent of disdain. A place like Mizner was never an option for them or most people they know, nor do I think it's something they'd crave. To them, it's more of a yuppie baby-boomer thing, ostentatious and wasteful. It's for idiots who cut into their life savings rather than living off the interest. I tend to agree with them—no matter how much money I have I'll always dress like a seventeen-year-old runaway. I expect to find the place pretty silly.

Walking through Mizner's demo homes, I'm stunned by what I see. It's not that the homes are impressive, though they are. It's what's in the homes. The Mizner developers have filled every demo home with personal touches: half-open cake mix boxes on the kitchen counter, photographs on the bookshelves, plastic shish kebabs on the Weber grill by the pool. It's insidious and fiendish; they're not just selling homes, they're selling identities. They're saying: *Here's who you'll be when you retire.* Unlike Vizcaya, where the homes have no personality, these homes have a ton of personality—just not your own personality. I spend a good hour walking around and scoffing at the ridiculous effort: the breakfast tray on the bed, as if anyone's cooking anyone breakfast, even in a state-of-the-art chef's kitchen. Upon closer inspection, the photographs on the bookshelves depict women showing a lot more cleavage than the typical granddaughter, and men who look a bit too much like black male model Tyson Beckford. Then there are the omnipresent photos of beautiful silver-haired men and women slow dancing, staring into each other's eyes. The message is clear enough: Enough with the Age of Menopause, the Era of Erectile Dysfunction. Don't you want to get laid again? Retire to Mizner Country Club!

But as I walk around, I start to feel less horrified. The house has a "men's study," which isn't so bad. Done in earthy, unpretentious mahogany, it has a tasteful nautical map of old-time Europe painted on the wall, and a neat-looking globe. I find myself thinking, *This is the kind of place where I could hang out.* I am horrified at myself, and try to shake it off. *Don't fall for it, idiot. You know what this study is. It's designed to make a retired fabric wholesaler feel like the CEO of Fiat.* In the guest bathroom, there are two used-looking towels on a drying rack. It is kind of cute, as if twin grandchildren have just tossed them there after rinsing sand off from their day at the beach. The coffee table in the TV room is the perfect distance for resting feet and watching golf. *Golf? You hate golf! When have you watched golf?!* And the poured concrete Roman pillars by the pool? That's pretty cool. To own your own pillars? I could get into that.

It shouldn't surprise me. I may dress like a seventeen-year-old runaway, but I still drink freshly squeezed OJ instead of frozen. I've spent fifty dollars on a haircut. I drive a Lexus, for God's sake. Who am I kidding? I stand in the great room for a long time, trying to deal with the fact that the first retirement option that truly speaks to me is a bona-fide douche-bag palace. So I just walk away and move on to the next place. I reject what I am feeling, stuff it deep away inside the great room of my subconscious. Perhaps I'll deal with it down the line, but I didn't come here to Florida to learn that I'm the kind of person who'd spend $1.2 million on a cake box.

VIVIAN

SLOW DANCING WITH OLD WOMEN is not something I've ever longed to do. No offense to my grandmother, but it feels a little unnatural. That's a fact I've had to confront ever since I started attending the weekly dance of the Singles Club of West Palm Beach. The club has for years been a life preserver for South Florida senior singles. I thought it would be interesting to visit it and see for myself how senior citizens romance each other. It didn't occur to me that being the only man present under the age of seventy would be like walking around with a sign that says "Yes, I will dance with you." I am automatically a novelty, like a dangerous greaser who shows up at an ISO dance. I am dragged to the dance floor, over and over again. The women clutch me to their party dresses and, as we sway, they hum along to the swing music. They're wearing perfume that smells like tea rose. It is the first time in my life I find myself wishing somebody would start the Electric Slide.

When I first see Vivian, she is standing across the room and staring directly at me. It's jarring when you catch someone staring and she doesn't look away like most people do when they're busted. Then, Vivian is beside me. She says nothing, simply stands and waits for me to acknowledge her presence. I don't know her at all yet, but I immediately sense we are in some kind of battle and decide not to give her the pleasure of an immediate greeting. I continue the boring conversation I am in and appraise her from the corner of my eye. She looks different from the rest of the older single women here. As women age they tend to start to look less distinctive. Their facial features soften and fill out, their hair becomes thinner and is coiffed into the ubiquitous old-woman Afro. Vivian, though, has somehow escaped that. Though Vivian must be in her early seventies, her hair is jet black, thick, and long. She has amazing posture. Her skin is tan and dark, her face is slim, and her features are sharp. She is the first old woman I have ever seen that I would describe as "sultry." She is possibly the sultriest older woman in South Florida.

"Aren't you going to ask me to dance?" she says. I've been the slow-dance slut of the singles club, but my heart starts beating fast and I feel that saying no would be the smartest thing I could do.

"I'm bad at dancing," I say, by way of an excuse.

"Yes, you are," Vivian says. "I've watched you; you don't know what you're doing."

She pulls me onto the dance floor and folds herself into my arms. Her posture is formal and bizarre-feeling. Her back is arched to an extreme. It's as if she has electricity running through her spine. As big-band music blasts from the hall's ancient speakers, I try to lead her around the dance floor, but really, she is leading. Periodically, she barks something like "Evolve! Evolve!" at me, and I have no idea what it means.

At some point, I become aware that I have an erection. The only explanation I can come up with is that I am turned on by how inappropriate it is to have an erection while dancing with an elderly woman. But that is circular logic. I have to angle my hips away from her so that she can't tell.

"I hear you are a writer," she says. "You should hear my life story. It will blow you away."

Vivian has an indeterminate Mediterranean accent that falls somewhere between Inigo Montoya and a discount electronics salesman. She is Romanian by birth.

"I am looking for somebody to write my life story," she says. "A writer like you. You are a good writer?"

"Yeah, I'm good," I say, more defensive than I want to sound.

"Just wait until you hear my life story," Vivian says. "It will blow your mind away. It has sex and love and passion. And a murder. It is better than a movie!"

Vivian hands me a business card. "This is my number," she says.

"Okay," I say.

"Good," she says. "I am looking forward to it. Maybe if you're lucky I will give you a dance lesson when you come visit me."

"Okay," I say.

She walks back into the crowd, and then I see the pairs of seniors all around, staring at me and whispering, and I feel odd and embarrassed and leave at once.

Vivian is very happy to see me, and guides me into her large condo. It's on a high floor of a prominent Palm Beach building. Her furniture is expensive-looking and large—the kind of stuff you see in luxury showrooms and wonder who actually purchases it. For instance, Vivian owns what I would call the most tasteful, most upscale animal-skin chair I have ever seen.

"This place is really nice," I say.

"Thank you," says Vivian. "Yet it is the least impressive place I have ever lived."

She's wearing tight black slacks and open-toed shoes with bright red nail polish. Her blouse is low cut.

"I'm sorry it's so hot in here," she says.

Vivian says that since she was a girl, she has always been crazy about movies; especially love stories. It's what made her want to come to America.

"My favorite movie is *Somewhere in Time,*" she says, pouring some wine. "Have you seen it? It's a love story. Who was the actor in that? The one who fell off the horse?"

"Christopher Reeve," I tell her.

"No . . ." she says. "That's not him."

"Yes, it is," I say. "It's Christopher Reeve."

"No . . . It is Reeves. Christopher Reeves."

"It's Reeve."

"Reeves," she insists.

I look at Vivian for a few seconds, and then I understand that she is a woman who has never lost an argument in her life, even when she was wrong.

"You're right," I say. "Christopher Reeves."

"That's what I said," she says. "That is his name."

"When I was a child," says Vivian, "I was nothing. I was ugly and nobody cared about me. Then I turned sixteen. I went to a dance and men asked me to dance over and over again, and I knew that things would be different. There were officers there from all over the world. One man said to me, 'When you get older, you are going to break all the men's hearts.' I thought to myself: I can't wait."

As Vivian tells me stories, she grows more and more animated. She smiles and leans forward and moves her hands more and more.

"I want glamour and passion," says Vivian. "Especially passion. Always I have known that. Other people might compromise, but I do not. If I do not have what I want, I move on from where I am and get what I want."

"You sound like quite a handful," I say, then, feeling nervous, I laugh.

"Oh yes," Vivian says, "I am. I am always testing my power. Do you like the music?" Soft classical music plays on the stereo.

"It's very nice," I tell her.

"Do you recognize the composer?" she asks.

"Rachmaninoff," I guess. I have no idea what Rachmaninoff sounds like. It just seems like something she would listen to.

"Correct," she says, smiling at me, impressed. She slides off her shoes and I notice that she has young-looking feet.

Vivian married for the first time when she was nineteen, to a man who promised to take her to America. But he took her to live in rural Delaware, which is technically America, but not the place she had in mind at all. Before long she had two children.

"Imagine me," says Vivian, "in the middle of nowhere with two young children!"

Vivian forced her husband to move to Hollywood, California, despite the fact that neither had ever been there. Desperate to keep her, he agreed. Vivian soon found herself courted by several wealthy Los Angelenos. She admits that she led them on and enjoyed doing it. She and her husband grew apart. When it seemed doomed, her husband flew out a close business friend to help broker a reunion between them. They all went to dinner. That man took a liking to Vivian and stroked her leg under the table. She had a small fling with him.

"I am a femme fatale," she says, with the sort of accent that allows you to pull off a statement like that. "I have probably hurt some men in my day. I know I have. I like the chase. I am like a man that way."

Vivian takes a deep breath, and I know in that instant that she would be smoking a cigarette right now if some doctor hadn't told her to stop smoking.

"It is interesting, no?" says Vivian. "Do you think I'm interesting?"

"It all sounds like a Jackie Collins book," I say. "Or maybe Danielle Steel."

"Why do you think I'm interesting?" she says.

"I don't know," I say. "You're not really like anyone I've ever met before."

Vivian smiles and leans back. I guess I said the perfect thing.

"I like talking to you," she says. "I like having a biographer. Ask me another question."

"How many times have you been married?"

"Six times."

"Did you end all your marriages?"

"All but the last," she says. "I met him aboard Papa Doc's yacht in Haiti. And he wanted me back the next day. Too bad I changed the locks."

Vivian takes a photo out and shows me, against all probability, an image of herself as a young, beautiful, comically tan woman, aboard the lavish yacht of notorious Haitian dictator François "Papa Doc" Duvalier. Her future husband stands next to her, his arm around her, dressed in white and looking like a studly Colonel Sanders.

I had assumed she was making this stuff up.

* * *

Vivian's apartment overlooks the Intercoastal Waterway, a sliver of water that winds down the eastern side of South Florida. We are watching it as we talk; it is burnished orange by a sunset.

"After I left my first husband I supported myself," Vivian says. "In the day I taught. At night, I worked in sex."

"You did what?" I say. I'm shocked, yet not surprised. Vivian is a sultry, sexy older woman. Why wouldn't all that sultry sexiness have a dark side? I consider that, and then I begin to wonder whether I am going to end up sleeping with Vivian. Horrified, I stuff that thought away, and then it comes raging back full force. Let's face it—this woman gets what she wants, she's been coming on to me, that is unmistakable, and now I have discovered she is a former sex worker. Whether or not I sleep with her might not be up to me.

"I worked in sex," she repeats. "Why is that strange?"

"It's . . . it's not," I say.

"It's a nice store, Sex Fifth Avenue."

"Saks Fifth Avenue," I correct her.

"Yes, Sex Fifth Avenue. That's what I said. I worked in Sex for two years."

I start to laugh. "Why is that funny?" she asks.

"Have you ever been in love?" Vivian asks me. We have moved to the living room.

"I don't know."

"You would know. Who are you dating now?"

"I'm not really with anyone. I'm really just getting back into the dating thing."

Vivian says she has been in love only twice in her life, and she married neither of those men. The last time she was in love was when she lived in Las Vegas. She fell for an ad executive. She was married at the time. In the beginning she and the executive would play chess together, and she'd beat him every time.

Eventually he invited her to his place. She began conducting an affair. She could see her lover's apartment from the regular table she and her husband sat at in their favorite restaurant. Her lover would flick his lights on and off when he knew she was eating there. Her lover was possessive and angry, convinced that Vivian was cheating on him with a third man. One time he came over and threatened her with a broken bottle.

"That turned me on," says Vivian. "I don't know why. I had the best sex with him."

"Why was it the best sex?" I ask, stammering over every word in the question. Vivian just arches her eyebrows, as if to say: If you don't know, then I feel sorry for you.

George was an American soldier who took a shine to Vivian and then proceeded to deflower her. He remained obsessed with her from that point on. He wrote her hundreds of letters. Vivian says he was the first man she ever loved, and the one she loved the longest.

"But he was never good enough," says Vivian. "He didn't have enough money or opportunities to keep me happy."

"If he did, would you have gone with him?"

"Maybe. But maybe it was less that I liked him and more that I liked that he liked me. Do you know what I mean?"

I think of every relationship that I've ever been in, and then I say, "Sort of."

One evening, Vivian invites me to visit her again. After we sit and have several glasses of wine, she asks me to read some of George's letters aloud to her. She sits back in her animal-skin chair with her eyes closed and a half smile on her face.

"I love you," I read. "I will always love you."

"You read well," says Vivian.

"Vivian," I read, "you are like a bull in a china shop. You kick everything to bits and then you shit on the pieces."

"He was a wonderful writer, like you," says Vivian. She's never read a thing I've written.

"What happened to him?" I ask her.

"He went to jail for murder," says Vivian, "and he died ten years later."

"Oh jeez," I say.

"He loved me until the day he died," says Vivian.

"I slept with a seventy-five-year-old woman," I tell Nick, my friend in New York, over the phone.

"You did what?"

"I slept with a seventy-five-year-old woman."

I've been telling my friends I slept with Vivian. I didn't really. It's another one of my weather balloons. I get to see how they would have reacted if I actually had slept with her, without any of the guilt of having gone through with it.

It's interesting to see how young people respond. Most find the idea so ridiculous they refuse to believe me. It's just not possible. My friend Jenni just snorts and says, "You're a bad liar." In the case of Nick, his reaction is several short, sharp intakes of breath, an awkward silence, a nervous laugh, and finally a troubled stamp of approval: "Dude," he says, "that's awesome."

Other friends of mine are openly disgusted by the idea of me sleeping with an older woman, which makes me a little angry; I feel like going ahead and sleeping with Vivian just to prove a point. Older women can be sexy. I have seen it with the Peppy Purple-ites, and I have felt it with Vivian. Shouldn't we all be happy about that fact? That we are not all consigned to adorableness?

Jill, my upcoming wedding date, doesn't really react well when I tell her.

"Man," she says, "you're just lost in the Amazon down

there, aren't you? With the cops, and the shuffleboard, and the purple people eaters or whatever."

"I didn't really sleep with her," I say. "I was only testing you."

"Yeah," she says. "Come back to us, Rodney! Come back!"

Most of the books I've been reading on health and aging make it clear that it's not just possible to enjoy an active sex life into your eighties and nineties, it's even recommended, as long as you are careful and cautious. A Duke University study found "a strong tie between the frequency and enjoyment of sexual intercourse, and longevity." A more recent British study had the same result, noting lower overall rates of mortality among men who have sex more frequently than the once-a-week average. The bottom line is: People who have "frequent, loving sex tend to live longer than those who don't."

What would it be like to sleep with an old woman? The books all write about "diminished lubrication" and a "thinning of the vaginal tissue." They warn that "some of the sexual positions you enjoyed at age thirty can be difficult and even painful at the age of seventy." So I guess the Wheelbarrow position is out. Sometimes I ask Vivian questions about sex. It's easy, because it's all under the guise that I am her biographer and interviewer.

"Oh, I don't have any of those problems," she says, waving her hand to dismiss the question. "I have better sex now than ever. I didn't know how to have sex until I was older," she says.

The next time I see Vivian she has moved in to a new apartment. She no longer wanted to live in the space she shared with her fourth husband. She wanted to start fresh. Her new condo is nice, but much smaller.

We sit down on the same couch. I ask Vivian how her love

life is going—we can do that now, we have broken down all those barriers. She tells me about a man who tried to pick her up in a fast-food restaurant, but all I can think as she tells me the story is: Vivian was eating in a fast-food restaurant?

Vivian's latest boyfriend is Italian, which is very Vivian, but he is the Italian-American blue-collar variety, not the Milanese one.

"I hate him," she says. "He's so ignorant. I need a smart man."

Vivian acknowledges that there's something nice about the simplicity of her new relationship. "I'm still in a world of dreams," she says. "But maybe I am stupid, because you can't have perfection. Maybe that's why my marriages didn't succeed. I didn't look for the good, I looked for the glamour, you know?" Recently she brought her new boyfriend to her daughter's for dinner, and Vivian was paranoid that everyone would be stunned by how far she'd fallen. But they loved him. "My daughter said, 'Isn't it time you overcame superficial things and went for something real?' "

"That sounds like good advice," I say.

"Yes, but 'something real,' it gets on my fucking nerves," she says. "I belong with younger men now that I am older. I am like a man that way."

When we finish talking, Vivian asks me if I want another glass of wine, but I decline and tell her I need to go. We stand and say good-bye at the door. I'm feeling nervous, and can't make eye contact. Do I shake her hand? A kiss on the cheek? But where on the cheek? And what if I'm wrong about this, if I've imagined the whole thing? I decide to give her a quick kiss squarely in the middle of the cheek. I do, but my aim is off, and maybe it lands a quarter inch closer to her mouth than I expect, and maybe I linger there a bit longer than a biographer should. Vivian doesn't seem surprised. The skin is wrinkled, but softer than I expected. Then I walk out, and Vivian does look surprised.

In the elevator, on the way down, I wonder to myself: Did Vivian look surprised because of my unexpected intimacy? Did she look surprised because she wanted more? Or did she look surprised only because it was such an unfamiliar sight, a man walking away from her?

GROWING OLD

You are as young as your faith, as old as your doubt, as young as your self-confidence, as old as your fear, as young as your hope, as old as your despair.

—General Douglas MacArthur, on his seventy-fifth birthday

BOB HOVER TEACHES MY ACTING CLASS. He's the retired soap opera actor, now in his seventies, living in the Sarasota area, who I became friendly with while playing senior softball. Years ago, Bob appeared as Dr. Russ Matthews on *Another World*. A lot of actors played Dr. Russ Matthews on *Another World* over the years, and I have met just one of them. But I am certain that Bob was the best. Bob just looks like a good Dr. Russ Matthews. Even in his old age, he has a deep tan, perfect hair, broad shoulders, and the kind of resonant, reassuring voice that would sound great saying the words "You have inoperable cancer." Maybe one in a thousand of us will look as good as Bob does at the age of seventy.

When Bob invited me to visit his acting class, I said yes

immediately. I don't have any interest in acting, or any need to see Bob outside our softball games. I said yes because Bob's class, as he had described it to me, is filled with aspiring young actresses from the greater Tampa area. Have you heard about the girls from the greater Tampa area? Probably a good 90 percent of the world's strippers come from there. Tampa is slutty!

I am also excited by the prospect of being in a room full of people who are around my age. That's because lately, I've been feeling a little strange. After four months in the retirement community, I no longer feel twenty-eight, or thirty, or even forty. I feel seventy. This, I believe, is because I am surrounded by old people all the time, and my mind has begun to assume that I, too, am an old person. It's the brain's natural adaptive instinct, the same instinct that causes me to start using a fake English accent every time I spend more than a few days in London. In Florida, that has meant that after a while I start to talk like an eighty-year-old Brooklynite. I say "hoid" instead of *heard*. Instead of saying "He's nuts," like I used to, I use old-timey phrases such as "That fella is lost in Yonkers!"

What's more scary is that at a certain point it transcends the mental and becomes physical. Listen to enough old men complain about lower back pain and you start to feel lower back pain. You begin to spend an inordinate amount of time wondering about your glucose levels. You notice smile lines on either side of your nose; *were they there before*? Am I experiencing age-related fat accumulation around my stomach, buttocks, and thighs? Is my heart muscle enlarging, as I hear it does when you age? Is my heart sheath hardening? That burning in my forearms: What *is* that?

And the worst of all: gray hairs. Gray hairs! I have found three now, three horrible gray hairs at my hairline. The other day, I saw one in the rearview mirror when I was driving and almost killed myself trying to pluck it out. I don't recall having any before I came down here. Are they leaping like mosquitoes from the heads of these old people and burrowing their way into my scalp?

The elderly people I hang around with don't make it any easier. They are terrible judges of age. Young people often think old people all look the same, but that misconception works both ways. To elderly people, young people merge into one tender pink blob. Elderly people always seem to think I am eighteen or nineteen, which is flattering until I remember that their eyesight is failing and that a certain percentage of them suffer from dementia. More than anything it's discombobulating, because you feel older than you are while everyone treats you as if you're younger than you are. What's doubly discombobulating is that I feel like an old person, but old people always say they feel like young people. So I feel old, but when you're actually old, you don't feel old. So I feel similar to elderly people, yet distant from them.

It's confusing. I'll spend the day like an old person, eating scrod and wondering if I should start stockpiling prescription drugs now, while I have the money. What if the prices get even higher? Then, at night, I come home and catch a glimpse of my young face in the bathroom mirror, and I'm always shocked: Is that me? Then, always, the shock is followed by relief: That *is* me! I am still a young person!

Three of the beautiful young aspiring actresses in Bob Hover's acting class are wearing tank tops. Two of the tank tops are camouflage tank tops. An army of women in camouflage tank tops could take over the world without much effort. Then there's a striking woman who is wearing a noncamouflage tank top. She is a conscientious objector in robin's egg blue. It's exhilarating being around such attractive young women after being away from them for so long. And as always, I'm amazed by the fact that it never gets any easier to talk to them. No matter how comfortable I get in my own skin, pretty young women always turn me into a teenager again.

"Rodney is a TV writer from Los Angeles," Bob Hover tells the class.

"It's nothing huge," I say. I shrug toward the tank tops, in a way that I'm hoping makes them think: That shrug had an air of mystery, maybe I will take him back to my dorm and sleep with him this evening.

"You a writer?" says one of the camouflage tank tops, sexily ignoring conventional grammar.

"Yeah," I say. I shrug again. It's starting to seem like a tic.

"I want to be a writer when I graduate," says the conscientious objector.

"You should see the stuff Christy writes," says Bob Hover. "It's good stuff. She's a good little writer."

"What school do you go to?" I ask Christy. "University of Tampa?"

Christy laughs. "I go to high school," she says.

"This class is for high school kids," says Bob Hover.

"Oh," I say, while I'm thinking: Motherfuck.

Before you label me a pederast, you should see these tank-top girls. I'll tell you what it is: Probably, girls mature faster in warmer climates, kind of like the way food ages faster outside the refrigerator. That's maybe why there are so many fourteen-year-old Brazilian supermodels.

Bob calls the class to order and says it's time for the first scene. Today the class is going to be improvising. That is, they will be acting out scenes off the top of their heads based on suggestions from Bob. It helps teach performers how to be fearless and act "in the moment."

"Would you like to be in this scene, Rodney?" says Bob.

"Oh no," I say, horrified. I hold up my notebook. "Just here to watch!"

"Oh, come on!" says Melly, one of the tank-top girls, smiling at me. "Are you scared?"

"Melly," says Bob, "why don't you join him up there."

"Okay," she says, and she bounds to the front of the room, flesh rippling her camouflage from beneath. It is the most patriotic thing I have ever seen. I stand and join her.

"Let's take a scene suggestion," Bob says to the rest of the class. "Where is this scene located?"

"High school!" shouts one of the kids.

"Okay," says Bob. "This scene takes place in a high school." He turns to us. "Give it a try, kids."

We turn to face each other. She smiles again. The fluorescent light glints off her see-through braces. I hook my thumbs into my pockets, because I have some sense that this will make me feel less nervous. We begin the scene.

"What's going on?" I say.

"Hey," she says, "can I talk to you, Principal Jackson?"

Now hold on a second here.

Principal Jackson? Why the hell did she make me Principal Jackson? I know I'm supposed to be acting, but I am too caught off guard by this development to respond to her. Do I look like a principal? Why would that be her first instinct? Why couldn't I be the captain of the hockey team, or the lunchroom rebel, for Christ's sake? Principal Jackson?!

"Um . . ." I say. "Um . . ."

"Principal Jackson, are you okay?"

I mean, really. Turn to the author photo right now. Do I look like a principal to you? At worst, I look like the young, good-looking English teacher fresh out of Vassar. The kind of young man who could wear a sport coat and a mustache and make it work. That's what you get for driving five hours to hang out with some chicks. They turn out to be underage murderers of the English language, and then they call you Principal Jackson.

The scene continues. I find it hard to listen to what Melly is saying because I'm too disturbed, so I just repeatedly tell her to "make sure her parents sign the permission slip," until Bob Hover has mercy on us and ends the exercise. For the rest of class, when I am not sitting in the back of the room sulking, he is forcing me to get up for scene after scene to play various authority figures. Bosses. Fathers. Priests. I mean, my God, one minute I was thinking of unpacking groceries from these girls' tank tops, and now I have to pretend to be their father? And for the first time in months, I remember that I am turning thirty in just over a year, and I think to myself: That *is* pretty old.

After class is over, the two camouflage girls leave. Through the window I see them get in the passenger side of tricked-out sports cars, driven by boys obscured by smoked glass. Christy, the conscientious objector, sticks around. She seems to have a crush on Bob Hover, which adds insult to injury. Unlike me, he is the kind of old guy young girls have crushes on.

"Hey," I say to Christy. "How old do I look to you?"

"How old?" she says. "I don't know. . . . I don't know. Do I get three guesses?"

Oh God. Everything has to be a game. How old are you? Sixteen?

"Sure," I say.

"Okay . . ." she says. "I guess . . . I guess. . . ."

I smile. Then I stop smiling because maybe it gives me wrinkle lines.

"I guess . . . thirty-three?"

I drive straight back to the Atlantic coast. It is dark, so I can't even see the swampland. I make it home to Century Village by three in the morning. By ten the next morning, I am poolside, surrounded by Shirley and the Pool Group.

"Hey!" they shout. "The kid is back!"

I lie down, marveling at how many years I'd be able to lie there before they stopped calling me "the kid."

Part Three

BASHERTE

BASHERTE IS YIDDISH FOR "SOUL MATE." All Jewish people have one. I did not learn that until recently, because I know next to nothing about my religion. That's become apparent over the last few weeks, since I began regularly eating breakfast with some religious Jewish retirees. The men go to synagogue every morning, and then to eat at Palmetto Park Bakery; they call themselves the Breakfast Club. Sometimes they'll talk about Jewish issues and I'll listen in. More often they'll crack filthy, racist jokes or make fun of me for being a twenty-eight-year-old without a girlfriend. They've invited me to attend services with them several times. I always make up an excuse, which according to *Successful Aging* is a bad idea. People who go to religious services tend to live longer than people who don't. Yet another way I'm screwing myself.

One of the men in the Breakfast Club is a retired rabbi from Connecticut. He has shiny, perfectly brushed white hair and a face in a permanent scrunch. He's a grouch who never disguises the fact that he thinks people like me are sapping the power from Judaism. He only talks to me when he's in a good mood, and when he's in a good mood he tends to lecture. That's how I learned about *basherte:* a Jewish husband and wife share one soul. It begins before they are born, when they are in heaven. When they are born, the souls are torn in half. It is not until they reunite and marry on earth that their souls are complete and shared once again. A person's other half is his *basherte,* or soul mate. It's a nice concept.

"So I have a *basherte,*" I say.

"Everyone does. Every Jew. Even you," says the rabbi.

"How do I find her?" I ask.

"You just do. It's meant to be."

"I'm almost thirty. Isn't it meant to be before that?"

"That," says the retired rabbi, "is because you aren't open to your faith. . . ." And then he's off again. He's in a great mood today.

I haven't met my *basherte* yet. Apparently you just "know," and up to this point, I haven't. That's scary, because I've met a lot of Jewish women. I grew up in the greater New York area. Jew Central. I have lived in Los Angeles: West Coast Division, Jew Central. I have been to Israel: Jew Central Classic. I have come in contact with a hundred times more Jewish people than my grandfather and father did before they met their *bashertes,* and I have yet to find mine. One reason for this, I think, is that I don't date Jewish women. In fact, I have never dated a single one.

"Does your *basherte* have to be Jewish?" I ask.

"What a stupid question," says the retired rabbi. "Of course they have to be Jewish."

"I don't really date Jewish girls."

"That's because you're always in church," says Harry Sloan, the loudmouth. The big joke at the table is that I am such a bad Jew that I'm a Christian.

"Look," says the retired rabbi, "if you don't date Jewish girls, then you are part of the problem."

"Your *basherte* can be non-Jewish," says Howard. Shy and quiet, Howard is always reasonable. He is not married anymore. "But she has to convert to Judaism," he continues. "The idea is that when the Torah was given to us at Mount Sinai, the souls of every future Jew were present. That included people that were going to convert. Her soul is already Jewish, even if she isn't."

"Don't try it," says the rabbi. "It never works. I've seen it a thousand times. Intermarriage never works."

"Why don't you like Jewish girls?" asks Howard.

"I don't know," I say. "They just don't do it for me. I just respond to different kinds of women. Exotic women."

"I think he means men," says Harry Sloan.

"Go with enough exotic women," says Arthur, "and your putz will fall off."

"Hey, hey, you know why Rodney likes going to Catholic church so much? You know why?" says Harry.

"No, why, Harry?"

" 'Cause all the priests there are homos!"

Then everyone laughs at me for a good ten seconds. I'll say this about old men: They know how to craft insults. It takes real insult know-how to slam someone simultaneously as both godless and gay.

I'd love to find my *basherte*. It would make everything easier. Everyone would be happy if I just found a Nice Jewish Girl, instead of, for instance, the last woman I brought home to meet the folks: a Moody Polish Girl Whose Ancestors Killed the Grandparents of Nice Jewish Girls. I can't control who I'm attracted to. It's the media's fault. When you're thirteen they serve you up Pamela Anderson. They serve up Heather Locklear. They tease you with Uma Thurman, who sounds Jewish but turns out to be Swedish. And what's the competition? Tracy Gold on *Growing Pains*? Melissa Gilbert on *Little House on the Prairie*? Look, if I wanted a girl with braids, I would go for a Swedish girl, or the hot Native American girl on the Land O' Lakes container.

"I think my *basherte* is one of those non-Jewish ones," I say.

"There's no such thing!" says the rabbi.

"Howard just said there was."

"He doesn't know what he's talking about." The retired rabbi looks at Howard, who looks down at his bialy, ashamed. "And I'll tell you something else," says the retired rabbi, "you don't find her cooped up in a retirement community with old folks. There are young Jewish women all over Boca. All over Ft. Lauderdale, all over Miami."

The rabbi is right. Over on the east side of town, by the ocean, there are plenty of younger Jewish girls. I take an afternoon off from retirement to investigate. I'll say this about Jewish girls: They really know how to take care of themselves. They really seem to like to hit the StairMaster. I spend a pleasant afternoon in an upscale mall, sitting on a bench outside Anthropologie and watching the Jewish girls walk in and out. I look at each one, sizing her up as a potential *basherte*. I stay as open-minded as I can. Maybe this one. Maybe that one. But doubt creeps in. I don't believe that my soul mate would ever have a desire to purchase overpriced candles. Later in the afternoon I end up in the Cheesecake Factory, trying to convince myself that the girl next to me is my soul mate simply because we both ordered Oriental-Style Lettuce Cups. But I know the truth: If either one of us was into dating Jews, we would have just ordered the cheesecake.

A more productive pursuit might be to look around for a non-Jewish *basherte* who would convert to Judaism for me. That's at least playing to my instincts. The best candidates seem to be the cute waitresses who serve me in restaurants. They're so smiley and helpful. They bring more ice water without being asked to. Someone like that might be open to Judaism. Then there's the olive-complexioned, not-Jewish girl who works at the Borders bookstore near my condo. Sometimes, as she is stacking up the Worst Case Scenario books by the cash register, she sings to herself in a soulful alto tenor. My infatuation is such that I am charmed by her collection of floppy, unflattering hats. She is friendly, but seems to want to limit our burgeoning relationship to financial transactions. I'm guessing that, in the thirty seconds it takes for me to buy a book, it's going to be hard to ask her if she's willing to consider converting to Judaism. Not that I haven't tried in my own subtle ways.

ME: Have you read this? [Pointing to display copy of a book called *The Joy of Oy*.]
HER: No.

Then I walk away. But if I really said what I was thinking it would be: "Trust me. You must trust me. I don't understand the religion myself, not at all, but it would make everything a lot easier if you could just go along with it. It will all feel right in the end." And she would convert right there, before she even rang me up, and she would throw in *The Joy of Oy* for free (or at least let me use her employee discount) and then, maybe, to commemorate that moment, we could go back into the employee break room and bone on top of remaindered novels.

* * *

JDate is the most popular online dating site for Jewish singles. Some friends of mine have been using it for years. Several of them have been urging me to use it down here in Florida.

"As long as you're staying down there," my friend Nick said, "you might as well get a girlfriend who's not ninety years old."

"Nick, I didn't sleep with that woman Vivian," I say.

"You keep saying that," Nick says.

I wasn't convinced about JDate until I met Al. Al is a retired eighty-three-year-old living down in Ft. Lauderdale. His body is bony and slight but he has a lot of energy. He lost his wife three years ago and since then he has gotten heavily into Internet dating. He maintains a profile on an assortment of dating sites, and spends up to four hours a day writing and reading e-mails from women all over the world.

"Do you get responses?" I ask. My limited experience with online dating sites has been this: You write ten or twenty letters to the hottest girls you can find on the site, and then none of them writes you back. Then, a few months later, a sixteen-year-old big-boned Goth girl in West Virginia sees your profile and cold-writes you, using so many abbreviations and emoticons you have no idea what she's talking about.

"Oh yeah," says Al, "I get lotsa responses. There's so many lonely women out there, you don't realize it. I got women from Russia, Bulgaria; I guess they want to marry an American. I had this woman, she was gonna come stay with me for a couple weeks from Russia."

"Al," I say, "I think that's a different kind of thing."

"Yeah," he says. "I saw she looked more like a man than a woman. I broke it off with her."

The rest of Al's online correspondence appears to be legitimate. The women seem to like Al; they write him as much as he writes them. He enjoys sending them lighthearted, lascivious e-mails. He'll ask them if they want to see a picture of him on the beach. Then he sends a phony photo of a bodybuilder naked on a beach with a sombrero over his groin area. Al keeps all the letters and digital photographs in a stack, and he lets me look through them. As I once again learn the extent to which old men get more action than me, I'm depressed. It's always better not to ask, but I always do anyway. Al walks over to his bed and points at the bedspread. He's the sort of older Italian guy who wears a lot of hand jewelry. "I have had sex with eight women on this bed," he says. Other than his wife, he has never slept with a woman that he didn't meet through Internet dating. Judging from the photographs, he is not a picky lover. He loves all women. The entire female species is his *basherte*.

"Do you believe in soul mates?" I ask Al.

"I already found my soul mate," says Al, gesturing to a framed old black-and-white photo of himself with his wife. "She's not here anymore. Now I'm just havin' fun."

Al hooks me up with a JDate account, and I spend the next few weeks staying up late and browsing it. It's no wonder it's caught on so much with Jewish people; using JDate is like catalog shopping. By reading each profile, you can learn an array of personal information about each woman: her name or nickname, where she's from, her favorite movies or books, what she is looking for in a man, what she learned from her last relationship. So you can rule out tons of people right off the bat. If they say they own a cat, they are out. If they say they like Billy Joel, they're out. That rules out, like, 75 percent. I do delay judgment if they specify Billy Joel's *Glass Houses,* which is a great and underappreciated album.

I join some non-Jewish dating sites too. On non-JDate sites, the girls don't tell you to write back, they tell you to "just HOLLA!!!!!!!!" They don't say "thanks," they say "THANXXX!!!!!!!!" Maybe the beleaguered history of the Jewish people has encouraged them to ration everything, including *X*'s and exclamation points. And the photos on these other sites: there is a lot of exposed midriff happening there. High-angle shots that enhance cleavage. Non-JDate girls always have the disembodied arms of their last boyfriend laying claim to them from the edge of the photograph. Tattooed arms. These are women that I'm not supposed to be dating.

"How's the quest for your *basherte* going?" the retired rabbi wants to know.

"It's going great," I say.

"Is she Reform? Conservative?" the rabbi wants to know. The rabbi is a Conservative Jew. He doesn't think that Reform Judaism, the most lenient form of Judaism, counts at all.

"She's Reform," I say, figuring that's the smallest lie I can tell. But that seems to disappoint him anyway.

Once you join online dating services you get even more junk e-mail than you got before. One afternoon JDate sends me an e-mail invitation for a "Jungle Party" they're hosting for members down in Miami Beach. This worries me; the Jews are not really a jungle people. But I've been feeling bad about not giving the Jewish girls a fair chance. And I like the idea of a big party full of Jewish singles. At least I'll be able to meet a whole bunch at once and let the law of averages work in my favor. In person, it would be a lot harder for them to ignore me like they often do my e-mails. My natural charm will take hold and then who knows?

The JDate Jungle Party is in downtown Miami Beach in a trendy club off the main drag of Lincoln Road. After months of understimulation, Miami Beach is shocking to me. I have been deprived of youth, and now there is a glut of it: short skirts, shaved heads, earrings, convertibles, Internet cafes, novelty T-shirts. There is something called Rock and Roll Sushi, which seems to be an ordinary sushi restaurant where they play AC/DC at deafening volume. (A digression: Al, the elderly Internet dating fiend, had an e-mail address that was ACDC@. . . .

ACDC stands for Al and his late wife's initials. He was baffled as to why he was always getting e-mails from young bisexual men.)

In front of the club, three huge bouncers sit outside checking names against the JDate list. They seem thrown by the experience of having to let in the sort of men they are paid to keep away.

The party inside is noisy and fashionably dark. It is so dark that I see nothing for several moments. My pupils dilate, and it is only then that the young Jewish women are visible. There are a lot of them. They were hard to make out because most of them have brunette hair and black party dresses. I'm struck by the massive hair-straightening effort that has gone into this evening for the ladies. It seems that every possible tool has been implemented to reverse the kink of each strand of hair. The men in the room are no different. Tankers full of hair gel have been deployed to hide every last bald spot. Basically, it's a party full of Jews looking for Jews where nobody wants to look Jewish.

Al had given me some advice on women that I found callous but wise. Al said that if you tell women what they like to hear, "they will do anything for you." He said that if I tell them that "I like that hairdo," or "Who did your hair?" or "I like those shoes," or "I love that handbag," they will eat it up. Al says I need to tell them they're doing something right. "Everyone likes to feel great." Al did not prepare me, though, for the possibility that I would have to unload these niceties in a room with dance-hall reggae blasting at over one hundred decibels.

Me: Hi! What's your name?
Girl #1: What?
Me: What's your name?
Girl #1: I can't hear you!
Dance-hall Reggae: I want to get it on till the early morn.

Me: I like your handbag!

Girl #2: What?!

Dance-hall Reggae: Girl, it's all good, just turn me on.

Some of my fellow Jewish men have ventured onto the dance floor, and there's no way I'm going to follow them. There's a reason why you never hear about world-class Jewish dancers. There's a reason why, in ancient days, we began picking people up in ballroom chairs and carrying them around. It's using furniture as a distraction. It's putting the focus on our real skill: upholstery.

I chastise myself for my negative attitude. Get a grip, I say. It's your negative attitude that keeps you from finding your *basherte*. Be positive. This party is a good thing. So many young Jewish people in one place, all looking for Jewish love. We know what we want: Jews. We know when we want it: now. It's time to stop fighting it. Get in there. Find her.

In a singles party, the challenge is to prove as quickly as possible that you are a big shot. You have maybe five to ten seconds of quiet in between songs. If you can't prove to a woman that you are a future Master of the Universe in that amount of time, you are lost. But I deliberately, adamantly, do not behave that way. I have faith. If my *basherte* is here, she will appreciate me for me.

A moment later, I am standing and talking to two women at once.

"Do you live in Miami?" one asks me.

"I live in Boca," I say. "In a retirement community." *This will be a conversation starter*, I think to myself.

"Oh my God," she says, her face bunching up. "You live in a retirement community? Like an old-person retirement community?"

"Yeah," I say. They seem weirded out, and I begin to feel panicky. "I wrote for Letterman," I say, apropos of nothing.

Another guy walks up to us. He looks at the two women and says, "Wow, you two look fantastic!" They smile and turn toward him, and I realize that I forgot to be nice and complimentary like Al said.

"You guys do look fantastic," I say, but the music drowns it out.

The party swirls around me, and I am an eddy in the middle of it. I am quietly furious. Furious at all the JDaters for being so materialistic, so superficial, and so not interested in me. A great thing to do, I decide, would be to go up to Jewish singles and share my Gray-dar with them. Gary-dar is an ability to predict what people are going to look like when they get old. Perhaps you are born with it, but it can also be developed, fine-tuned, especially if you spend a lengthy amount of time living with elderly people. You start to notice the correlations between the facial structures of young and old people. I could walk among these singles and tell them how their bodies are going to riot against them. I could say to a woman: "Hey, you look great. I just want you to know that you're going to be able to open cans with that nose when you're eighty." Or I could walk up to a guy and say: "Get ready for hunchback!"

At this point, I've entered the foul sort of mood in which you're better off not talking to people. I just wander around, and by wander around I mean I drink three vodka rocks in rapid succession. A woman at the bar starts a conversation with me. I try to steady myself.

"Are you going on the JDate bus trip tomorrow?" my *basherte* asks. A potential response enters my head that I recognize would be a horrible thing to say. I wait for a new comment to replace it in my brain's on-deck circle. My brain is not cooperating, so I just say:

"JDate bus trip. I hope it doesn't get attacked by PDate."

"What's PDate?" she says.

"It's, uh . . ." I try to think of something different to end this. I cannot. "It's uh . . . it's Palestinian date," I say.

My *basherte* walks away. I finish my drink. I am drunk.

One day I go to synagogue with the Breakfast Club. I am the youngest person at morning services by at least fifty years. I hardly know the prayers, so I just do that thing you do when you don't know the words to a song: You sing the syllables you do know as loudly as you can, and mouth the rest. The sections I remember tend to be the sections that sound most like curse words—that's what happens when you memorize something at age thirteen.

"Shee———it!" I sing.

After services we go to breakfast. I am on the rabbi's good side now, so he lectures at length.

"How was that dance you went to?" Howard interjects.

"Tell us this," says Harry, "did you have sex? Are you having sex?" Talk about thirteen-year-old boys.

"No," I say, and they all groan, even the rabbi. "It's hard," I say. "It's hard these days."

"Well, if it's hard you should be using it!" shouts Harry. Bedlam breaks out.

"Keep the faith," says the rabbi, as rabbis must say all the time. "You'll find your *basherte*. Everyone does."

I wish I had that faith. It had been a long drive back to Boca from Miami that night, and I had thought a lot about what had happened. The truth as far as I can tell is that I just have some block against Jewish women that for now is insurmountable. Wherever my *basherte* is, her half-a-soul will have to float around for a while.

The most reasonable explanation I can give is that a relationship with a Jewish woman is a far more real relationship than I am prepared to deal with right now. Once I decide, I'm stuck, and then next thing I know it's fifteen years later and we're at our triplet sons' bar mitzvi, and she's yelling at me in front of the entire extended family because the caterer just dropped the ten-tier cake shaped like a movie robot.

A relationship with a non-Jewish woman is like a vacation. It's short, it's exciting, it's different, and if I want I can go home afterward.

"Actually," I tell the Breakfast Club, "I met somebody online last night."

Here is what I don't tell them: She was not half of my soul. In fact, she was half Cuban, half Puerto Rican, and she loves David Sedaris. I was not charmingly modest. I told her my book was exactly like a David Sedaris book, and we have a date next week.

NICKELED-AND-DIMED

ONCE RETIREES RETIRE, it's not uncommon for them to want to unretire. They've made it past the initial stages of adjustment, and now they're experiencing the onset of restlessness, not to mention residual guilt over the perception that they do nothing productive all day long. Myra, who works as an activities clerk in the Century Village clubhouse, has unretired three times.

"Every time I retire I realize I'm not happy doing nothing," she says. "I get a job. I'm not the kind of person who is happy sitting around." Almost 20 percent of Americans over the age of sixty-five are still in the workforce in some capacity. Some of them are there because, like Myra, they prefer working. Others are there because of financial considerations (like my roommate, Margaret, teaching piano). *Successful Aging* says that it's good for elderly people to continue working and feeling productive in some capacity, even if it's volunteer work. Although to be honest, I'm starting to get a little sick of that book and its whole rah-rah attitude. It seems like if you did everything that book says you need to do to age well—exercising; staying mentally sharp, socially active, religiously active; volunteering or working part-time to feel productive—you would drop dead of exhaustion. Maybe, I'm thinking, *Successful Aging* and the MacArthur Study is some scheme by the government to kill off elderly people so they can skip out on our Social Security debts.

I've been retired for almost four months now, and I'm not sure that I feel like unretiring yet. David, my manager, called the other day to tell me I had a job offer on a TV show.

"They want you to start in two weeks," he said. "Back in Los Angeles."

I thought hard about it. Part of me feels drawn back to the working life. My gut tells me that the only natural place for a twenty-eight-year-old is in rush-hour traffic at 8:45 A.M., switching from lane to lane with a lukewarm cup of Starbucks rising from between his legs. But I still have some money saved. I don't have to work just yet.

I call my friend Nick to talk it over with him.

"I think you should take the job," he says. "You're in a rut down there."

"I'm not in a rut," I say, "I'm in a groove." Nick snorts. "I feel like if I left now," I continue, "I would be betraying the experiment. Part of testing retirement early has got to be toughing it out. It's not like the real retired people I know down here can just get up, turn young, and go home."

"You just want to stay down there because you're boning that old lady," he says.

"I didn't," I say. "That was just a test to see how you

would react. I was exploring attitudes toward elderly sexuality."

"I don't believe you anymore," he says, laughing. "Take the job. You've gone bananas."

I call David and turn down the job. He's not happy. He makes 10 percent of what I make.

"I think you're making a mistake," he says. "You're in your peak earning years. You're going to fall off the radar down there if you're not working."

I've decided to take a job. I'm going to be working part-time in the Palmetto Park Bakery, one of my early bird breakfast haunts. I want to experience what work life is like for retired people who decide they don't want to be retired anymore. I am surprised that the bakery is willing to let me work, since the only experience I have with baked goods is that I sometimes eat muffins. But they hire me for some reason. Well, maybe the reason is that I'm willing to work for free, and they are calling my job "observer," but add, "maybe we'll let you do a few things."

"I'll send you ten percent," I e-mail David and then I add a smiley face, but he still doesn't write back.

Palmetto Park Bakery is a typical South Florida bakery. There are three or four elderly waitresses, hired because of their low cost and ability to interface well with elderly customers. Then there are a few quiet, hardworking Haitian busboys and cooks, who send money home to their families (and also, Sherman tells me, keep local mistresses on the side). Sherman works the bakery counter. He's a temperamental older man with black hair and a propensity to yell. One funny thing about Sherman that I've noticed is, when customers mistake him for the owner of the restaurant, he doesn't correct them.

At first, they want to keep me out of the way. I'm the change supervisor. My entire job is to stand behind the cash register waiting for the moment Sherman is running low on one-dollar bills. Nobody writes about it, but apparently there is a huge singles shortage in South Florida. I suppose they're all tucked into birthday cards and sent to grandchildren in Great Neck.

When Sherman tells me we're running low, I have to go annoy Vicki the waitress, and ask her if we can use her tip money as customer change. Vicki tells me to go ask Terry the waitress. Terry asks me to go ask another waitress, Ann. Ann, acting put out, says she's out of singles. Before I started working at Palmetto Park Bakery all the waitresses seemed like sweet older women, but now they intimidate me. I usually get too scared to be pesky, and I have to run outside in the heat to the adjoining businesses and beg them for singles instead. It's a lot of moving around for someone who has been sitting on his butt for four months. But that's the great thing about working, I'm remembering; it gives you lots of reasons to race around and feel useful, as long as you don't think about how asinine your use actually is.

I'm shocked by how much some of the employees here rag on elderly people, especially because most of the employees are elderly people. One man asked Sherman if coffee was free. Sherman told him that it was not. As soon as the man was gone, Sherman started to bitch: "Coffee for free? Where can you get a bagel and butter for eighty cents and he wants a coffee on the arm too? They nickel-and-dime you, complain about it when we raise prices a few cents."

"He seemed nice to me," I say. I know a lot of the customers on a personal basis; the Breakfast Club, for instance.

"Rodney," says Sherman, "if it was my business I'd tell him to go screw himself." He then reaches out and, for punctuation, flicks me very hard on the ear, as if we are both Little Rascals.

"This one time," says Terry the waitress, "I saw a lady put a glass in her purse."

"I'd say ninety percent of our Equal packets are stolen," says Belle, the greeter. "And half our silverware. They treat this place like their own pantry."

"Assholes," says Sherman.

Sherman will go on tirades like this within earshot of the restaurant owners, which seems insane to me. After talking to the owners, though, I learn that they're even more burnt-out than their employees.

"We opened the restaurant with the best intentions," Mabel, the co-owner of the bakery, told me, "and within three days I had been reduced to tears."

Ever since those tearful early days, Mabel has kept an exhaustive and obsessive log of the daily indignities she suffers. One day she gives it to me to read. The following is my summary of it:

JANUARY 2002:

Old male customer asks for a bagel and the counterperson gives him one from the top basket.

Old man: "That's not what I wanted—are you stupid?"

Counterperson: "No, I'm not, and who do you think you're talking to?"

Old man, who has somehow obtained a cup of water, defiantly pours some on the ground.

Counterperson: "That's great, sir. I expect that from my kids."

Old man throws the rest of the water in the counterperson's face and bolts.

APRIL 2002:

Old man comes into the bakery and, for some reason, begins to belt out Sinatra songs at the top of his lungs. Customers bothered a great deal. Owners ask him to stop. He does not. Finally, an elderly customer walks over and chokes him. It takes two guys to pry him off.

LATE AUGUST 2002:

Massive cane fight in bakery area.

OCTOBER 2002:

Old man drives off, forgets to take wife with him.

DECEMBER 2002:

Elderly customer: "What's your name?"
Mabel: "Why?"
Elderly customer: "Nice to meet you, Why!"
Customer calls Mabel "Why" for rest of month.

"It can't be this bad," I tell Mabel.
"Give it a few hours," she says.

After I have proven myself competent at overseeing dollar bills, Sherman lets me handle the bagels. He briefs me. First: We have to handle the bagels with a fresh plastic bag over our hand or elderly people freak out. Second: There are twelve different varieties of bagel and bagel stick. Third: Always repeat their order, and remember to speak up.

"Lastly, always tell them they're getting 'the fresh one,' " says Sherman, "even if they're not."

Another new responsibility is that I must make sure that everyone's bottomless cup of coffee is full. If a customer sees white at the bottom of his cup, he starts to gripe. So I have to dance around, making sure nobody is seeing white. It's like being trapped in the lamest video game of all time. I can't believe how much coffee elderly people drink, by the way. What do they need to stay alert for? They can nap all day and no one cares.

The customers rarely make eye contact with me or say thank you. These are the same senior citizens who talk my ear off poolside. Somehow I am less worthy of their conversation once I am in a subservient position. They save their friendliness for the waitresses and just push their mug out toward me. Or they look down and watch me pour, which sucks because for some reason my hand always shakes, and I tend to splatter a little coffee around. It's all way more pressure than it's supposed to be. If I wanted to get run ragged and yelled at, I would have taken the job my agent offered me.

More screwups: I botch some take-out orders. It's little things, like bringing regular cake instead of sugar-free cake. It turns out that this is a big deal to people with adult-onset diabetes. A couple of times, while I'm handling bagels, I forget to put a plastic bag on my hand. Customers refuse to buy them. That drives me nuts. There's a complimentary bowl of day-old cake on the counter, and customers seem to have no trouble touching *that* with their bare hands.

At the end of the shift, I walk, exhausted, out into the midafternoon sunlight. An unexpected pleasure washes over me that I haven't felt in a long time. I'd forgotten the best part about working: how it feels when you finish working. The relief. Relief is the closest thing to happiness I know. I miss that feeling. In its own twisted way, it's the best argument yet for going back to work.

Maybe, after forty years, when you finish working you don't feel a great sucking void in your soul. Maybe you feel an intense, once-in-a-lifetime sense of relief and satisfaction that only forty years of hard work can earn you. Most of the people I hang out with down here in Florida earned their retirement. They aren't beating the system like I am. They put in their time. I know guys here who served on their sanitation department for forty years. Or they worked at the same stationery company for an entire career. I know one guy, Larry Beck, who managed to be a salesman, a real estate mogul, a Hawaiian politician, a nudist colony owner, and a Catskills entertainer. He never stopped working; he's a millionaire, and he seems happy.

I turn to Sherman, the counter guy, as he wipes down the counter.

"Hey, Sherman," I say, "how did it feel when you were done working for a living?"

He looks at me like I'm a moron. "I'm not," he says.

Then Mabel comes over. She pats me on the shoulder and says I did a great job and that she hopes I come back, as a customer, to eat.

"You seem to be implying I can't work here anymore," I say.

"Pretty much," she says, and that's when I decide to re-retire.

FOR MY BOOK

I GET TO THE BAR EARLY. My date picked the place; she lives nearby. It's a nice-looking, lively bar in North Miami Beach, on the site of what I believe used to be a decrepit old bank with a flaking mural of Dwight Eisenhower. The whole neighborhood, in fact, is looking much nicer than when Grandma lived here.

This is the kind of luck I have with blind dates. They end up occurring in places where I can point to a window thirty yards away and whisper: "By the way, that's where my grandma had her fatal stroke." Then the seduction can continue as I put my arm around my date and take her for a romantic stroll around the neighborhood to see: the Denny's that my grandmother always called "Danny's"; the movie theater that we saw *Platoon* in, when Grandma fell asleep and I sobbed beside her; the wide strip of beach that I would spend each afternoon on, getting poked and prodded by an endless succession of Grandma's elderly female neighbors; and the streets I used to putter on afterward, toward the video arcade, flip-flops flopping, sunburn deepening, and sand up my ass in a too-tight bathing suit.

Then the romantic stroll ends at the bottom of Grandma's building. On the buzzer board, the Jewish names have been replaced by Cuban names. You can still see the faint outline of my grandmother's name on the board. Death and Migration! It will be the perfect moment to try to kiss my date. I will try to kiss her and then I will notice that she left over an hour ago.

This is the first blind date I've managed to wrangle since I moved to Florida. My first few months here I hardly met any women my age. Then I hit upon a strategy that significantly increased my ability to talk to women. I started asking them out For My Book. That's what I told myself: that it doesn't matter if they reject me because I'm only doing it to generate material. No matter what happens, it is For My Book. I recommend to everyone that they have a book that they can say they're doing things for. It really gives you a renewed sense of bravery.

For My Book I asked out random women all over. Mainly I asked out waitresses and service people who have to be friendly to me because it's their job. I asked out a pretty Indian salesclerk right on the floor of a Staples superstore. She had a very nice ring, I noticed, on the third finger of her left hand. Turned out she was married, unfortunately. Then, For My Book, I chatted up a waitress at the Palm Diner. She had quit her last waitress gig because "there was way too much meth and Oxy going around the kitchen, and I can't be around that stuff." Sounded hot to me—I asked her out. She gave me her phone number in front of her emotionless Greek boss. Then, For My Book, I called her three times in the next two days, leaving increasingly exasperated messages with her roommate. She did not call back. This stung a little, because this girl was heavyset with an infected pierced nostril.

For My Book, I asked out about thirty girls on the Internet. Twenty-five of them never wrote back. The one date I got out of it I am on tonight, and now I have Grandma's ghost as a chaperone.

Inside the bar, I fret about buying a beer. I don't want to be tipsy when my date shows up, but I also know that alcohol will calm my nerves. Why do we make dating so hard for ourselves? Blind Internet dates? It makes no sense to buy into something sight unseen based on unverifiable claims. You learn that when you're a kid, on the beach in Florida, and the X-ray specs you ordered turn out to be bogus. And yet, here I am. I know next to nothing about the woman I am meeting. I know that she is half Cuban and half Puerto Rican. I know, based on her first name, that she is probably not Jewish.

Christina!

I know from her online profile that Christina loves David Sedaris, which means that I have some vague sense that my approach should be to present myself to her as a hetero David Sedaris. What will she look like? I have no idea. Her photograph online was of her large, dark left eye. Her thick, angled eyebrow poked in from the top. When someone hides behind a "creative" photograph online, that is often an indication of bad news ahead, so I am expecting the worst. But part of me remains hopeful, because it is a nice eye—sexy and well-mascaraed. When I picture myself in bed with the giant eye, it is not an unpleasant fantasy.

Senior citizens should have no problem falling in love, when you think about it. Logic dictates that seniors should fall in love even more easily than teens fall in love. When we were fourteen, we had love figured out. We had crushes on people we could see and smell, who got us excited. Smart, huh? In fact, falling in love should be even easier for seniors because there's much less pressure than there is for teens. You are eighty. You have presumably felt boobies. Also, you've completed your career, raised families, and done the whole "for richer or poorer till death do us part" thing, for better or worse. The hard part is done. It's all muffin tops from here on out.

So why is that not the case?

Amy Ballinger, my ninety-three-year-old stand-up friend, says it's the men's fault. "Single male seniors are animals," she says. "Whatever stage of arrested development they were in forty years ago when some woman grabbed them up, I now have to deal with that unfinished business. They haven't changed; they've just been married for forty years."

I've spent a lot of time down here talking to single elderly men, and I have found that Amy is understating things. Single elderly men may be the most immature population on the planet. I've heard them say the kinds of things that in a football locker room might be considered "going too far." I've been to a strip club with old men. Strippers always think it's great when a cute old man comes to a strip club. But that's only until the cute old man begins to flagrantly ignore the club's "no hands" policy. Then the strippers give you the skunk eye because they think you brought the pervert, when it's the other way around entirely.

Every morning a bunch of guys who call themselves the Bullshit Club meet in the clubhouse social area of Century Village. Rumor has it that the Bullshit Club is just a cover for the men's shared passion for illegal sports betting. That may be true, but they still spend two or three hours each morning telling one another sex tales. Men have a genetic disposition to blab every time they get laid. It's funny: women get the bad rap for always wanting to talk after sex, but at least they want to talk to their partner, not all their betting buddies.

The pattern is that one guy tells his sex story while the other guys try to prove he is lying.

"I've had seven broads in five weeks!" Frank will say. "You should have seen the last one. Tits, ass! She got a figure like a movie star! She had all the goodies!"

"Your nose is growing," says Mo.

"She put out?" says Ed. "She wasn't one of those dinner ho's?" A "dinner ho" is an elderly woman who dates men only to get them to take her out to a nice dinner.

"She made me dinner!" says Frank. "Fuckin' baby lamb chops!"

"That's bullshit!" says Mo.

"She's very orgasmic," says Frank.

"These older women," Ed tells me, "they're very sexually oriented. You can play with 'em, they still come. They love oral sex!"

"Yeah?" I say.

"Oh yeah."

"And you can, like, still perform?" I say, which shuts the Bullshit Club right up.

"I can perform," says Ed.

"Bullshit!" says Mo. "Every night?"

"Every night?" says Ed. "Well . . . not every night."

"They always try to get you to their place," says another

woman I've met down here, Lee Ravine. "They say they want to show you their apartment. And not just to try and sleep with you. These men have an inordinate amount of pride in their little apartments. They want to show off their rental furniture."

When a man gets too frisky, Lee says that she gives him a pamphlet on AIDS. She tells them that senior citizens are one of the fastest-growing populations of HIV carriers in the United States. They tend to leave soon afterward; nothing douses arousal like an AIDS pamphlet, she says.

"Men are idiots," she says. "Nothing personal."

Christina shows up at the bar, and she is very, very attractive. Her skin is the same color as the dark beer I am drinking. She reminds me of several wooden, big-breasted fertility statues I used to see in the Museum of Natural History when I was a kid. I don't tell her that, and I don't tell her about my grandmother's stroke; I don't tell her about a lot of things, I just buy her a beer and smile like a loon, amazed at my good luck.

She seems more nervous than me. "I've never been on an Internet date before," she says. "Have you?"

"No," I say, and I decide that another thing I should not tell her about is For My Book, and how I've asked out about three zillion people online in the last two weeks.

"I haven't been dating that much since I got here," I tell her. "I've been too busy with my book."

"Are you going to write about this?" she asks me.

"Oh, you know . . ." I say, getting uncomfortable, "I might want to write something about Internet dating or something, but . . . you know . . . I'm not gonna write about, like, specific people."

"Internet dating creeps me out," Christina says. "That's why I just put up a picture of my eye. I don't need a million strange, lonely guys ogling my breasts."

I smile, focusing on her dark eye, not her breasts, her thatched eyebrow, *not her breasts, her breasts, her breasts, her breasts.*

"Yeah," I say, "you don't need that."

One of the women in the Pool Group, Barbara, is having trouble finding a man. That's surprising to me because she's a trim, pretty, older woman with curvy features and a good head of hair. One day Barbara asks me to set her up on some dates. "You're meeting so many men for your interviews," she says, "you might as well get me some phone numbers." That's the kind of luck I have—I go to a state full of Jewish yentas and somehow end up setting *them* up on dates.

Once I begin looking for dates for Barbara, I see how few suitable men there are. I find one elderly gentleman for her down in Ft. Lauderdale, but Barbara wants to date only Jews. My hunch is that this man is not a Jew, as he is named Fritz. So I build Barbara some online profiles on several Jewish Internet dating sites. I ask her the questionnaire items while we sit by the pool and enter them into the computer later. We sit far enough from Shirley and the rest of the Pool Group so that we can't hear their conversation about local omelet deals, and they can't hear what we're doing and make fun of us.

"How old should I say you are?" I ask her.

"I want to say I'm in my sixties," she says.

"How tall?"

"Five foot three. But I think I'm shrinking. But don't put that."

"What kind of man are you looking for?" I ask.

"I'm not fussy," she says. "Just a man who is smarter than me and taller than me. And prettier than me."

"Okay."

"I don't want to sound vain," she says. "Of course I am vain, but they don't have to know that."

"Okay."

"He has to drive! I'm not going on the bus with him! No more of that."

"Check."

"Tall, dark, and handsome. He has to be sweet and gentle. Into good health. A walker. Nonsmoker. I don't even want to be near a smoker. And he has to be single. Not married."

"Okay."

"But he doesn't have to show me his wife's death certificate; some of these men have done that to me. That's poor taste."

"Okay."

"He should want to go shopping with me. And he should be a good dancer. And I don't want fat. No fatties! Slim! I once had a fatty! Friends set me up! We had dinner out on the Island, thank God. I was hiding!"

"Anything else?"

"He should be wealthy. And wise!"

"Okay."

"I'm not fussy. Anyone will do, really."

How do any of us end up finding anyone? It's a miracle if it happens. Everyone throws up their own dopey roadblocks. And then there is the tyranny of freedom, as evidenced by Barbara: we have so many options that we become incapable of settling on any of them, and become too picky. We run the risk of never finding anyone. In the old days, it seems like it was easier.

"When I was a kid," my friend Norm told me, "you married the best-looking girl in you neighborhood who would sleep with you right after the ceremony."

Christina and I are drinking beer and talking, and it is going well. I am fighting off all nervousness. We are smiling at each other, sitting close together and riding the swell. She is tapping her fingers on her beer bottle. The song on the jukebox is so cheesy, but somehow it's perfect: *"I want to know what love is! I want you to show me!"* says the jukebox.

"Who actually picks this song, for real?" says Christina. Christina is a few years younger than me and just moved back to Miami from Brooklyn. She grew up about four blocks away from where my grandmother lived. Now she's living at home again, and it's a nightmare. For years her parents didn't care where she went or how she behaved, but it's different now that she's under their roof again for the first time since high school.

"You're Jewish, right?" she asks me.

"Yeah."

"I used to always crush on the Jewish boys in high school," she says. Her high school was half Jewish. She spent a lot of her childhood at Jewish homes, lighting Chanukah candles with her friends.

"There are Jewish Cuban people too," she says.

"Are they called Juban?" I ask. It's supposed to be a joke.

"Yes, they are," she says, and we both smile again, and she is so pretty and moody, which I love, and so Cuban, and I am so Jewish, and perhaps we are both picturing our big-nosed, well-mascaraed little Juban babies, and . . .

"I want you to show me!"

. . . I wonder to myself: Am I attracted to pretty, moody girls because of my romantic, artist's soul, or is it because I'm a Jew, and dating a beautiful, flawed woman is just good bargain hunting?

None of the men who dates Barbara ever call her back. She has no idea why. I fear it might have something to do with the fact that we lied about her age on her computer profile by at least ten years. Most older men online seem to want women who are younger than sixty-five, so we fudged even more than I expected we might.

"I'm disappointed," she says, "but one still might call. He's not home from vacation yet, I don't think."

Barbara has an impressive, impossible, inspiring, positive attitude. She wants me to get right back on the horse and start finding her dates again. I suggest that maybe she should join a different online service, to freshen things up. A younger one. She wants to join the one that I am on, Nerve.com, which typically appeals to twenty-three-year-old New York City libertines who need to be inside a crashing automobile to get off.

"Okay," I say, running the questionnaire, "they want to know your turn-ons and turn-offs. Tattoos?"

"Ugh, forget it!"

"Body piercing?"

"Oh God, no!"

"Long hair?"

"No!"

"Flirting?"

"Yes."

"PDA? Public displays of affection?"

"Holding hands is okay."

"Uh . . . erotica?"

"What's that?"

"I don't know . . . pornography, sort of."

"Oh . . . kinky things?"

"We can move on."

"That's okay. Say yes."

"We can move on."

"I love this! This is like I'm seventeen again!"

* * *

Christina and I are drunk now. I am driving with her. We are a little too drunk to be driving. The roads are empty. It's late.

I am pointing at all the spots I used to frequent when I visited my grandmother. She is pointing at the same spots and telling me how they figure in to her own life.

That's the Denny's we used to get lunch at.

That's the Denny's she used to get lunch at.

That's the movie theater I saw *Platoon* in.

That's the movie theater she used to get drunk in back of.

That's the beach I was pinched and prodded by old ladies at.

That's the beach she would go to with her boyfriends when her parents were waiting up.

She wants to know: "When is your birthday?" She has her window down so she can get some air. I tell her December.

"Oh God," she says, "Sagittarius."

"What's wrong with Sagittarius?"

"Sagittarians always break my heart," she says. "You can't pin them down. They're cheaters."

That's the sort of comment you need to ignore when you are seriously thinking about kissing somebody.

In front of her house I shut the car off. Her parents' bedroom is in the back but her mom can hear a car idling from a mile away. How odd to be simultaneously afraid of someone's parents discovering you and worried about whether you'll be able to get up in time the following day to make your shuffleboard tournament.

We talk and I am quite sure she is waiting for me to kiss her. And why shouldn't I? What do I have to lose? But a kiss is meaningful, so I start to think about everything that kissing her would mean, and then I just try to ignore the conversation in my head, and I kiss her. And then we stop kissing, and she looks embarrassed, and looks toward her house, and says,

"Maybe we should go someplace." And I smile, and I am embarrassed, and then she says, "Maybe we shouldn't." We sit there for a while, and then we decide what we are going to do, but you cannot know what, because some things are not For My Book.

THANKSGIVING

THREE DAYS BEFORE THANKSGIVING, I let the cat out of the condo. It was a genuine mistake; I was taking some trash out to the chute and left the cat guard open for about forty-five seconds. When I returned, both cats were in the condo, present and accounted for, as they always are. The cats had never shown the slightest interest in the outside world. Like Margaret, they seem to prefer life inside the condo, so I had stopped being quite so meticulous about keeping the guard shut all the time. If anything, I thought I was providing a service: letting a little fresh air in for half a minute to thin out the cat smell.

Apparently, in the forty-five seconds that I was gone, mayhem occurred. Ranchipurr ran out the door, down the hall, and sat for a moment on the welcome mat of the condo next door. This was at the same moment that our neighbor was opening her door to get the morning newspaper. The woman was frightened badly. She gasped and shut her door, convinced she'd seen a wild raccoon. She called Bill the Building President, hyperventilating. All buildings in the retirement community have a president, elected by the residents. They're generally seen as former business executives who can't exist without a title of some kind. Bill asked her to look outside again and see if the raccoon was still there. She peeked out her window, and watched Ranchipurr—yes, it is definitely a cat, she realized, not a raccoon—step off her welcome mat and slink back into our condo. Then a few seconds later I came sauntering past, wiping garbage residue on my pants.

Later that afternoon, Bill the Building President came to visit Margaret. It was unexpected, and she didn't have time to hide the cats and birds. Bill informed Margaret that the cats and birds were against community code, and had to go immediately. Margaret began to protest, explaining that she needed the animals to keep her company after the untimely passing of her husband. Bill explained that he was aware that she had lost her spouse before moving in and had cut her some slack because of those circumstances for several years. At this point, though, he must take a stand and enforce the code. Margaret's animals had to go, or, if she insisted on keeping them, then she must go.

So that's bad. What kills me is that things had been going well. Day to day, Margaret and I had also been getting along better than ever. She never nagged me to practice the piano, which I appreciated, since we live together and that could have gotten awkward. If anything, I reminded her to practice, since playing the piano always seemed to put her in a more cheery mood. It was a cute little dynamic we had: a piano student nagging his teacher that she's never going to get better if she doesn't play between lessons. One afternoon I came back from a jog and from outside the condo, through the closed Plexiglas blinds, I heard her practicing. I couldn't believe how gorgeous it sounded; for a moment I thought it was a CD. She really is a phenomenal pianist. Rather than enter the condo and interrupt, I jogged another loop and let her do her thing.

Since Bill the Building President's visit, though, Margaret has been spending each day pacing and fretting. Every couple hours she asks me again if I'm the one who left the cat guard open. I always lie outright and say that I wasn't. She must see right through it. How else would the cat have gotten out? But I don't see how it would be productive at this point for me to admit the truth. It won't change the situation. It's not like Bill will absolve Margaret if he finds out that it was my fault. Technically speaking, Margaret's housing me is against code too.

Feeling guilty, I offer to drive around looking for communities that Margaret could move into. She agrees, since I'm the one with the car. The requirements are that the community must be pet friendly and have access to public transportation. I spend a day looking for her new place, revisiting Vizcaya and other places I'd looked at for myself. A number of communities fit her criteria, but what I learn is that they tend to be newer communities catering to younger retirees and families. They're much pricier than Century Village, and Margaret will never be able to afford them. I end the day without having found a single viable option that allows pets. I try to put a good face on it for Margaret.

"There's lots of solid options," I tell her. "You'd just need to bring the animals to a humane shelter, and then you can finally get involved in the community here. It could be like a new start for you."

"I just want to live here," she says, "with my pets." I've

read that's common; once elderly people are settled, they are loath to move.

"But that's not possible, Margaret," I say. "You have to be practical."

"Maybe Bill won't come back," says Margaret.

"He's going to come back," I say.

"Maybe he won't," she says.

I could have left Florida for Thanksgiving and gone north to New York. My family was begging me to get out of Century Village for a few days and come home. Thanksgiving is my favorite holiday. I have dinner with my extended family, and then I go out with all of my old high school friends who are also home for Thanksgiving. We get drunk and go cruising around to all the old high school hangouts. Now that we're pushing thirty years old, it's starting to feel a little pathetic to be smoking a joint or doing whippets in a 7-Eleven parking lot. But I still love it.

In retrospect, going home for Thanksgiving would have been smart. I never would have left the cat guard open and this mess would never have happened. Too bad I thought it would be a good idea to see what Thanksgiving was like in the retirement community.

But it turns out that many of the residents fly north to New York so they can be with their families. My usual crews—my bus friends, the Shuffleboard Club, the Bullshit Club, the Breakfast Club, Amy Ballinger—are all gone. Shirley from the Pool Group told me she would be around—she even promised me we could play canasta together—but, predictably, she's disappeared from the pool area now that the rest of the Pool Group is away. I haven't seen one of those mysterious ambulances around the community in days, so even death has taken a long weekend.

The residents I know who are remaining here are all visited by their families from New York. The overall vibe is like Parents Weekend at a college, but instead, it's the kids visiting the parents. There are rental cars and grandchildren everywhere. All the grandkids seem to be named the same thing. The swimming pool is overrun with Brandons and Chloes going apeshit in the water. The forty-year-old parents yell at them to stop splashing, and they yell at the grandparents to stop telling Brandon he's "strong" because it encourages him to splash. Later on, you hear one of the grandparents whisper something like: "When you first named her Chloe I didn't get it, but it's grown on me."

On the night of Thanksgiving, everyone disappears to go eat their family meal at the Cheesecake Factory, and Century Village becomes a ghost town. It's eerie. I end up calling home to my family twice in two hours, just to feel like I'm a part of it all. I can hear the clamor of my extended family in the background. I miss my sister, and my dad and my mom. I even miss the way my uncle Larry always observes that my hairline is beginning to recede, which I don't agree with.

"So, Rodney," my mom says, "did you find someone to eat Thanksgiving dinner with?"

"Totally," I say, "totally."

"What's Margaret doing?" she asks.

"I'm not sure," I say.

"Are you going to invite her out?" she says.

"I should," I say. "You're right, I should."

I get off the phone. She has a point. It's probably a good thing I'm down here now, since I can keep Margaret company while she's bummed out about losing her husband and now her cats. But, for that very reason, I feel like avoiding her altogether and celebrating Thanksgiving on my own.

The sun is going down, and I have no idea where to go. I'm baffled. Where is everyone? It can't be that they just go inside for the night and wait it out. Where do unaccompanied retirees go on Thanksgiving?

The mystery is solved when I walk by one of the Century Village synagogues and look through the windows. There are about two hundred residents eating Thanksgiving dinner in the main party room, at large circular tables. It looks like a pretty swell time. On their plates, I can see fluorescent light bouncing off glistening turkey skin. Someone is playing dance music on a synthesizer. I feel a sudden urge to crash the banquet, and figure why not? I'm crashing everything else down here in Florida. Maybe I can bring some food back for Margaret and the cats and get on their good side for a few hours.

The banquet organizer sees me as soon as I walk in and makes quick work of extracting forty bucks from me. He starts marching me across the dance floor, trying to find me an empty chair. The whole place seems to be watching us. He sets me down at a big table near the kitchen, saying, "There's a guy your age at this table, you'll have a lot to talk about." The guy he's referring to is a man who looks to be in his mid-forties, with thinning hair and gym-rat muscles, which makes me feel less than great.

Everyone at my table is from Long Island. Sitting next to me on my right is Sylvie, a vivacious and plump woman in her early seventies. The young forty-five-year-old man turns out to be Sylvie's son, Keith. I'm worried at first that they're just going to ignore me, the stranger, but in fact, the opposite happens. It dawns on me that I have found the perfect place for this evening. I've found a table full of elderly people who wish that they could be with their grandchildren. Everyone at the table begins to lavish attention on me. Everyone wants to know where I'm from, what I do, how I like Florida. Sylvie in particular takes a liking to me. She's an elderly woman with a sweet disposition that puts me at ease.

"Oh," she says, soon after I sit down, "I get handsome young men on both sides of me! Aren't I a lucky one?"

I smile at Keith. "How you doing?" I say. "Pretty good," he says. He's the one person at the table who seems less than thrilled with my arrival. Maybe he's wondering why a random young person would be eating alone at a retirement-community Thanksgiving banquet. But my bet is that he's threatened by the fact that I'm now the resident youngster at the table, and he's no longer the center of attention.

"A writer in our midst!" shouts Sylvie when she finds out what I do for a living. She turns to her son. "A writer, Keith!"

"What kind of writing do you do?" says Keith. "Have you ever had anything published?" I pick up on his cynical tone so I start to embroider my writerly accomplishments.

"Oh!" shouts his mother. "A TV writer! How exciting!"

"Do you write for TV shows we would know? Like *ER*?" asks one of the tiny old women.

"Yes, just like *ER*," I say.

"I'm in real estate development," Keith tells me. I didn't ask.

"Have you seen a lot of stars?" Sylvie asks me.

"Sure," I say. "I see them all the time."

"I only develop in Manhattan, though," says Keith. "That's where the money is."

"Have you ever seen Paul Newman?"

"Sure," I say. "Ol' Blue Eyes!" Is that even what he's called?

"Ohhhhh!" says Sylvie. "That's exciting!"

Keith looks down at his plate and grits his teeth. I don't blame him. I'm committing Grand Theft Mother, directly in front of him. I don't feel bad about it. Why should I? It's been a rough week, and I need to borrow a mom right now. And judging from how fast Sylvie latched on to me, Keith isn't fully satisfying his mother in the son department. I am just taking advantage of the opportunity.

A server brings me a plate of turkey. It's not bad. Sylvie and I continue to talk, as Keith concentrates on his food.

"Hey, Rodney!" says Sylvie.

"Let him eat, Ma," says Keith.

"Hey, Rodney," says Sylvie. "I'm looking for a new condo. I rent now—I know, dumb—and I'm looking to buy. Are there any condos open in your building?"

"I'm not sure, Sylvie," I say. "Do you want me to check for you?"

"I'm looking for a two-bedroom," she says. "So Keith has somewhere to stay when he comes to visit."

"I'll keep my eyes open."

"What about single men?" says Sylvie. "Are there single men in your building?"

Keith snarfs on his salad. "Ma!"

"What? I'm just asking."

"I'd be happy to help you out," I say. I am being nicer to Sylvie than I am to my own mother. "Did you lose your husband?"

"They're divorced," Keith says, glaring at me.

"We're divorced," says Sylvie, sighing.

"That's the age we live in," says a tiny woman across the table.

"But lucky for Keith," says Sylvie, "my ex lives in the community next door. Isn't that lucky? So he can visit both of us when he comes down. Right, Keith?"

"That's right, Mom. It's very convenient."

"Rodney is going to find me a real catch," says Sylvie. She spins back to me. "Find me a podiatrist!"

"Why?" I ask. "So you can get free consultations?"

"He can start at the feet," says Sylvie, "and then work his way up."

Keith puts down his fork. "Ma! Enough!"

"I'm just kidding with Rodney," says Sylvie. She turns back to me. "Find me a boyfriend and a condo, and you'll be my hero." She adds, "You can stay in the extra bedroom and work on your book! Then when Keith comes down, you two can share the room!"

"That's nice of you to offer," I say. "But for now I already have someplace to live."

"Where do you live?" Sylvie asks. "Maybe we live in the same zone."

"I live in Essex," I say.

"Oh!" says Sylvie. "That's not where I live. But that's where she lives!"

Sylvie motions at Evelyn, the tiny woman across the table.

"Which building do you live in?" Evelyn asks.

"I live in building D," I say.

"Me too," says Evelyn. "What floor?"

"Ground floor."

"Me too," says Evelyn. "What number?"

"105," I say.

"I live in 106," says Evelyn. "We're neighbors!"

"What are the odds of that!" exclaims Sylvie.

"Did you say you live in 105? With the lady with the cats?" says Evelyn.

"Yes," I say. "With Margaret."

"One of those cats nearly scared the life out of me the other day," says Evelyn. "It was sitting right on my mat! I had to call the president and complain!"

My jaw drops. Unbelievable.

"Oh my God," I say. "You're that woman?"

"What do you mean, 'that woman'?" she says.

I don't know where to begin. It's just too weird a coincidence. How do things like this happen? There are thousands of people in this community, and I end up sitting at a table with the woman who snitched on the cats? It's hard not to interpret it as some kind of sign from above. I was sent to this table for a reason.

Dinner is cleared and the one-man band begins to play again. I plan what I can say to tiny Evelyn. Sylvie stands up and puts her hand on her son's shoulder.

"Keith," says Sylvie, "I want to dance."

"Go ahead and dance, then, Ma," he says. He motions to the floor, where lots of elderly women are dancing together.

"Do you want to dance with me?"

"I gotta go to Dad's soon, Ma," he says.

"How do you like that," Sylvie says to me, making a joke of it. "He won't dance with his mother! I bet Rodney will dance with me!"

"How about this," I say. "I'll dance with Evelyn, and the two of you dance together."

"I can't dance," says Evelyn, "I have clubfoot." She points to her foot, but it just looks like a foot to me.

Sylvie grabs me by the hand and pulls me onto the dance floor. The DJ is playing "Boot Scoot Boogie." She's an enthusiastic dancer, like many of the women I've met here in the community. I keep looking over at Keith, sitting at the table, talking to nobody. I regret stealing his mom at this point. I was only trying to steal the good part of his mom; he was supposed to keep the irritating part. I'd forgotten that they cannot be separated.

Finally, Keith comes over and steps in. "Okay," he says, "one dance before I go to Dad's."

I go back and sit at the table, but Evelyn is now engaged in conversation with another, tinier woman, and I can't break in. Keith returns to the table after the shortest mother-son dance in history.

"Nice to see you all," he says. "I'm going to visit my dad." He pointedly does not make eye contact with me.

"Are you going?" says Evelyn. "Can you give me a ride home? I don't want to walk."

"Of course," Keith says.

"I'll give you a ride home!" I blurt, with way too much enthusiasm.

"That's okay," says Keith, "I'm leaving now."

"I'm leaving now!" I say.

"What," says Keith, smirking, "and let down all these ladies on the dance floor?"

"Stay, stay," says Evelyn.

I put some food in a napkin and stand up.

"Trust me, it's fine, I'm leaving."

"Geez," he says, shrugging, "be my guest."

My drive home with Evelyn is about a quarter of a mile long. The first eighth of a mile, we are silent. Then Evelyn speaks up.

"What's it like, living with her?" she says. "She's a nut, huh?"

"Margaret? Not at all. She's a really great woman."

"That's not what I've heard."

"No, I live with her. She's shy when you first meet her, but she's pretty special when you get to know her. Have you ever heard her playing piano?"

"What, you think I'm not going to hear her through those flimsy walls?"

"She's amazing, isn't she?"

"You're not supposed to have musical instruments like that," Evelyn says. "She's disrupting the peace, it's against the code."

It's starting to seem a little crazy to me, the way they run these places. Pets and pianos are against code. Meanwhile, it's okay for everyone to have garish, oil-painted seascapes and the ugliest sofas you've ever seen.

"You know Paula upstairs?" Evelyn says.

She's talking about Paula the Pool Group gossip. Sure I know her.

"Paula said that woman, Margaret, is giving piano lessons too, and you can't do that, you can't run a business out of your condo. She has no respect for the rules, the one you live with."

We're pulling in to our parking lot. Evelyn has clubfoot, which is lucky for me, I guess, because walking her to her door will buy us a final minute of conversation before the opportunity is lost.

"Can I tell you something?" I say. "I let the cat out of the condo the other day."

"You let it out? It nearly scared me to de—"

"I know. I'm sorry. I'm a bonehead. Margaret is so good about keeping them inside. She got them just before her husband passed away. I think they keep her company. Are you married?"

"No," Evelyn says. "My husband passed away in New York, before I moved down here."

"Oh," I say. "That's the same as Margaret. The same thing happened to her."

"Yes," says Evelyn, "but you don't see me breaking all the building rules because I miss my husband."

"Good point," I say.

"I don't know how you live with her," she says.

"It's not that bad," I say. "And I think things will settle down as soon as I leave."

"She's good at piano," says Evelyn, "that didn't bother me so much. It's just those cats."

"They're good cats," I say. "Very well behaved. You won't see much of them after I go, I promise."

"How do you know?" she says.

"She's thinking about getting rid of them," I say, which is an out-and-out lie, but maybe it will buy Margaret some time for this thing to die down.

Evelyn thanks me for the ride, and we enter our adjacent condos. For the record, Margaret never hears from the building president again.

When I go inside, I see that Margaret has fallen asleep in front of Animal Planet. She wakes up when I come in, and I give her the food wrapped in the napkin. She thanks me and takes it into the kitchen to warm up. It feels like the most pathetic good deed of all time; you try giving an old woman a bunch of food in a napkin and see if you feel good about it.

I go to my room and spend the next three hours watching parade highlights on TV. Jesus, as always, knocking on the door. Maybe I should have brought Jesus food in a napkin too. It was a nice night, I think to myself. I met a lot of friendly people. Everyone was on good behavior. It's reassuring to know that, if you're old and retired and don't know many people, you can still have a good time, and it doesn't even require an act of mother larceny.

I decide to call some of my high school friends to see if they're out for the night in our hometown. I reach my friend Nick. There's a loud pounding bass drowning him out.

"Where are you?" I ask.

"We're in the city," he says. "We decided to come back here. Nobody felt like hanging out in Scarsdale or sleeping in their parents' house."

"Aw, man," I say. "That used to be the fun part. You guys can't make changes like that without asking me."

"Yeah, well," he says, and then he trails off.

The phone gets passed around, and I talk to everyone as I pull off my clothes and get ready for bed. It's been a while since I've talked to most of my friends, and there is a lot to catch up on. Between the pounding bass and the loud whir of my ceiling fan, they all sound so distant, and in that moment I wish they were all a lot closer. I step out onto the patio by the bird so I can hear better.

"Everyone misses you! Do you miss us?" my friend Eva yells.

"WHAT'S UP, MAN?" says the bird. And then, eight hours early, the bird adds, "BEEP BEEP BEEP BEEP BEEP BEEP BEEP BEEP!"

"What?!" shouts Eva.

THE SUNSHINE STATE

SOMEHOW, AGAINST ALL ODDS, I ended up with a golf buddy. He's a sixty-three-year-old former heroin dealer named Artie. For thirty years he checked out of workaday life. He lived abroad, summering in Italy and wintering in the Indonesian isles. I met him because he was briefly my real estate agent when I first got to Florida.

He was an off-putting real estate agent. Off-putting even for South Florida, a region with a vast share of America's most off-putting real estate agents. This might have a lot to do with his low level of professionalism, such as his habit, while showing condos, of repeatedly using the phrase "Check this shit out!" Then there's his annoying tendency to forget to mention pertinent features of his properties: peeling paint, musty odors, or, in the case of one condo he showed me, a South Asian man sleeping on the floor who Artie says comes with the apartment.

Within seconds of meeting me, Artie figures out that he and my father are from the same Bronx neighborhood. In fact, Artie graduated from the same high school as my father. Artie, of course, uses this as a pretext to continue calling me with must-see condos, even after I informed him I had found a condo in Century Village.

"Come on," he would say, "just check the shit out. Whaddya wanna live with an old lady in a shoebox for? Throw me a bone. We're from the same neighborhood!"

One evening, Artie calls me on my cell phone and asks me if I feel like playing golf with him on his day off. I say yes. There's something I like about Artie. He reminds me of the Bronx side of my family—the side that always tanned more easily and smelled like cologne. I've been told that it's common in South Florida for new retirees to gravitate toward people from their childhood neighborhoods. That's part of the reason older New York retirees end up living in big Bronx-style condominium buildings and baby boomer retirees prefer living in suburban-style tract homes; they're re-creating the environment of their youth.

Before I arrived in Florida, I'd largely considered golf a sport for marketing executives. I had no interest in it. But playing golf with Artie feels subversive to me, what with his potbelly and his unkempt mustache and his insistence on saying things like:

"A good golf shot, kiddo, such a rush! It's like the first time you try dope, you know?"

"Dope as in . . . weed?"

"No! Dope as in dope! Heroin! Like the first time you try heroin, you know?"

The golf is a nice break from the retirement community, as ridiculous as that sounds. How sad is it to need a getaway from your getaway? People back home are starting to give me a hard time about how long I've been down here. It's been way longer than anyone expected, including me. Months longer. I've been here in the retirement community since July 4. Almost half a year.

When I talk to people back home on the phone, they're starting to get passive-aggressive and judgmental.

"You've been down there a while, haven't you?" my agent said to me the other day. "I hope you haven't *really* retired!" Later that day, my dad told me, "You think maybe it's time for you to start thinking about going back to Los Angeles and getting another job? Unless you've *really* retired!" Everyone always thinks they came up with that joke.

Why am I still here in Florida? I have no idea. I came down here to check retirement out forty years early. Almost six months later, any sane person would say I have accomplished that. I now understand retirement on a visceral level. I know what it looks like: chaise lounges, thunderclouds, midsized sedans, tile floors, and ear hair. I know what it sounds like: tennis ball thwocks, ambulance sirens, slot machine bells, and parrots. I know what it smells like: chlorine. I know what it feels like: terry cloth.

I understand retirement on a deeper level too. It's not just that I can now pronounce the word *colonoscopy*. I understand Florida retirement on a level that actual retirees may not. I realize now that retirement is not just a bunch of old people sitting around and waiting to die. They do other things in addition to that: clubs, jobs, sports, acting classes, and countless hours spent sharing cruel gossip about neighbors.

Why am I still here in Florida? Part of it may be inertia. At this point it would take more effort to leave than to stay. It's not as if I have a job back in Los Angeles, or a girlfriend, or any compelling reason to go home. I've wired Florida up pretty well at this point. Down here, I know how to feed myself. I have a sock drawer. I have a golf buddy. I'm living well for less than thirty dollars a day. True, I am jarred awake every morning by an African gray parrot imitating my alarm clock. But what would morning be like without that parrot? Would the silence be unnerving? Should I just stay here indefinitely and savor what I have? After all, the president keeps warning that the Social Security system is going to be overhauled. This could be the only retirement I'll ever experience.

Why am I still here?

I don't take full blame for the situation. The elderly people down here have to accept partial responsibility. They have let me down. If they had held up their end of the deal, I might have left long ago. You see, elderly people are supposed to be wise and inspirational. They are supposed to reinvigorate us with a newfound appreciation of life's value. I've seen *On Golden Pond* and read *Tuesdays with Morrie.* I know how it's supposed to go. If I met my own Morrie, he and I would share uplifting deathbed rap sessions deep into the night. The nurse would come to the door and say, "Aren't you two getting tired?" and he would laugh a wheezy laugh, wave her off, and launch into another compelling anecdote about making love to a Russian lit grad student while inside a canoe. He would give me life lessons. He would give me marching orders. He would coax me out of my rut and send me back home.

But I haven't found any Morries down here yet. I've met some intelligent, charismatic older people, but nobody I'd want to hang with all the time. Most people get annoying after a while. I don't think *Tuesdays with Morrie* would have been so uplifting if that guy had to spend more than Tuesdays with Morrie. By Thursday he would have been cursing Morrie out.

Why am I still here? I met a woman in Palmetto Park Bakery the other day who told me that "Jewish people need signs." I related to that immediately; it was almost wisdom. That's exactly what I'm doing at this point. I'm waiting for a sign that it's time to go home. Then the woman handed me a Jews for Jesus pamphlet and told me I could still be Jewish if I accepted Jesus as my savior. I thought to myself: I don't need Jesus to be my savior. He is already my roommate.

I've been seeing Christina a few times a week. I suppose she's a girlfriend, of sorts. Yet another reason to stay in Florida. It's a weird relationship. She's a twenty-six-year-old who lives with her conservative Cuban parents, and I'm a twenty-eight-year-old who lives with an elderly roommate in a retirement community. It's impossible for us to spend a night together. Does that count as boyfriend/girlfriend? It feels way more old-fashioned than that to me, like we're a-courtin'.

I love going to visit her. I drive on the causeway over Biscayne Bay, toward the twinkling condominium lights of North Miami Beach where she lives. It's not just leaving Century Village behind; it's leaving *everything* behind. Miami Beach exists in a wormhole where the 1950s, the 1980s, and the 2000s are all existing at the same time. The other night, a Lionel Richie song, "All Night Long," came on the radio as I drove over the dark water toward the city. I was elated. The only way it could have been better is if I had been wearing an unbuttoned white linen shirt that billowed in the wind. *Hey! Jambo jumbo!* The whole trip, I decided, was worth it, just for that moment.

It's exciting just to be around a young woman again. The air between us is thick with anticipation. Because our relationship seems to exist out of time and place, I don't worry about it. Christina takes me to Cuban restaurants and orders for us in Spanish. Much like Jane Austen characters, we chastely eat pizza on Collins Avenue. We hold hands on a municipal bus. It's discreet and cute, just how I want it.

"Have you slept with her yet?"

That's what the guys in the Bullshit Club want to know. Is it strange that sometimes I want to tell eighty-five-year-old men to just grow up? Before I tried retirement I might have expected old men like this to respect my romantic idyll. I bet that Morrie from *Tuesdays with Morrie* would have. But now I know that most old men won't rest until penises are filling every void on earth. It's a fact of life. The idyll must end; the boning must begin.

My friend Chuck from the Bullshit Club gave me a Viagra pill. It was sky blue and quite enormous.

"It's from India," he said. "A generic."

I take it one evening, when I am out with Christina at *Lord of the Rings: The Two Towers.* I was curious what the effect would be. Chuck warned me that the pill takes a while to kick in, so I pop it with a handful of popcorn an hour into the movie. Within twenty minutes, I notice that I can no longer breathe through my nose. It occurs to me that Viagra must make every membrane fill with blood, not just the wiener. I end up having an uncontrollable erection throughout the entire Battle of Helm's Deep. It is fueled by my anxiety that Christina will somehow misinterpret it, and think that I am aroused by Orcs.

After the movie, as always, I drive Christina home to her parents' house.

"My parents want to meet you first," she says.

That seems hilarious to me. We are grown-ups. We are two consenting young adults in Miami Beach, and at least one of us is gooned on wine, Cuban food, sildenafil citrate, and an oversized box of movie Goobers.

"I want to meet them now," I say, half serious. I check the dashboard clock. It's two in the morning.

"It's too late." She smiles. "Next time." She says good-bye and gets out of the car, and I drive off thinking: *This could be a sign.*

* * *

I want to play canasta before I leave. I've decided to fixate on it. I've done everything else there is to do in Florida. But not canasta. Canasta may be the key.

You can't just walk in and play canasta. You have to be invited. It's an unbreachable citadel, like the elderly woman version of Skull and Bones. Women play head games with me about it. They invite me to play with them, then, on game day, the phone call never comes.

Even the rules of canasta are shrouded in mystery.

"How do you play canasta?" I ask Shirley from the Pool Group. We're sitting in deck chairs and watching some of our neighbors swim slow laps in the water. Shirley is the worst with the invitations, always bailing on our canasta dates at the last minute. But, because she's the one who got me into the Pool Group, I'm still counting on her to get me into canasta.

"Oh, there are so many rules," she says, "it's better just for you to see."

"When can I see?"

"Oh, anytime," she says, as if she hasn't been saying that for months. "I'm going away for a while, and then I get back. Then we'll have a game. Soon."

"Should I buy a book in the meantime? So I can learn how to play?"

"Oh no," Shirley says. "There aren't any canasta books."

"Of course there are canasta books," I say. "I've seen hundreds of them in Borders bookstore."

"Oh, they're no good," she says. "Every game of canasta is different. Every one has its own rules. The rules can change from year to year. They're always changing."

"But there must be standard rules."

"Oh, sure, there are standard rules," she says.

"Great," I say.

"But not really," she says.

* * *

Artie's golf swing is powerful but sloppy. In fact, his whole golf persona is sloppy. His shirt is always untucked, like the corner of a too-small fitted sheet. He chain-smokes on the course. In the Pro Shop, the cashier seemed to want to delouse Artie's credit card. It didn't help that Artie informed me in front of the cashier that he'd bought his golf clubs from a "junkie in SoHo" for twenty bucks.

When it's my turn to take my first golf shots ever, Artie overwhelms me with pointers. I can't keep track of it all at once. According to Artie, I'm supposed to bend my knees, not swing the club too hard, keep my feet apart, keep my arms straight, keep my "fuckin' eye on the ball," and "hit down on the ball." Also, I'm supposed to relax.

"If you get uptight," says Artie, "you're not gonna hit right."

"I'm trying to relax," I say. "It's hard with all these things you keep telling me."

Artie himself is a terrible golf player. He invariably slices the ball. He's lost three balls by the time we're on the third hole. But he looks good with the ash hanging off his cigarette. I'll give him that. He's not a bad golf coach. He's very encouraging, even when I get frustrated. And when I manage to remember all three hundred pointers and launch a real golf shot in the air for the first time in my life, Artie forces the foursome in back of us to join him in a very enthusiastic round of applause for me.

"Hey hey hey!" he says. "Tiger Woods!"

The best parts of golf, I feel, are the parts where you're not actually playing golf. The golf cart, for instance, is a lot of fun. Artie floors it, and we seem to be able to drive wherever we want. Artie steers us up steep grades, and down into grassy green gullies, and then spins us in a couple of pointless circles. As we cart around, we try to one-up each other with stories about our lives. I exaggerate a great deal. I make writing for Letterman sound even more exciting than writing for *Your*

Show of Shows. Then Artie tells me amazing stories about his years abroad that obliterate my beefed-up stories. Artie and his wife, Sandra, lived like royalty. Artie would travel to places like Thailand and Afghanistan "before the Russians ruined it" to score massive amounts of heroin. Then he would fly back to Italy or Bali, wherever they happened to be living at the time. They'd sell the heroin and use the heroin and have tons of money left over for throwing parties.

Artie is nostalgic about everything. The way they never had to wake up until noon. The way they lived right on the water. The way he used to go hot-tubbing with Danish girls. The way you could trade dope for coke. The way he and his wife used to take their shits in rustic holes, and after they were done, pigs would come and eat their shit.

Artie makes drug-dealing sound harmless. Back then it was easy to smuggle. You just had to pour the dope into special hollow-framed bags or, worst-case scenario, shove the drugs up your rectum (Artie demonstrates the rough size and shape of an ass-drug ball by holding up a few golf balls). According to Artie, using heroin for thirty years also has incredible health benefits.

"Oh yeah," he says, "on dope you age a lot slower. You never get sick. It kills the germs or something. Thirty years, I never got anything. Well, I got hepatitis C. But everyone I know has hepatitis C."

Against all reason, I am smitten with Artie's description of his life. It's hard not to be jealous of the guy. It's a way more hard-core version of my retirement experiment. Artie and his wife retired before they ever went to work. They just checked out and said screw it. They had an amazing time. Why would you ever need to retire if you lived like that?

I've called in a favor. The mother of an L.A. friend of mine lives in a neighboring retirement community, one of the rich ones. Through my friend I arrange to attend her mother's regular

Friday-morning canasta game. I'm finally going to storm the canasta citadel. For a few days beforehand, I gloat about it to Shirley and the Pool Group, who have never come through for me on the canasta front. I don't tell them that the women aren't going to let me play yet. They've only agreed to let me watch. I'm pledging the sorority.

"You're going to Bridgepoint?" Shirley says, her eyes widening. I can tell she's jealous. They're all fascinated by Bridgepoint, because the community is so much more well off than Century Village is.

"I hear they got a heck of a clubhouse," she says. "I hear they got three or four card rooms for just a few hundred people."

"I hear they play canasta for money," says Bea.

"I'll let you know," I say.

My hope is that the jealousy seethes in them for a while, and they end up inviting me to play with them. You have to be patient and strategic if you want to break into the canasta scene. It requires more of a bridge sort of mentality.

For the first half hour of my Bridgepoint canasta game, nobody even mentions canasta. I begin to fear that the entire retired female gender is conspiring to mess with my head. The four women all talk at the same time. They show one another photos of their grandchildren and then they show one another photos of their grandpuppies. They gossip about other women in the community. "Have you guys seen Jan?" asks Judith. "She just got back. Face full of Botox. Everywhere."

It is as if I am sitting inside an episode of *The View,* but this episode is hosted by four Barbara Walters and I am the only audience member. Dottie tells me that she is "the slut of the tennis courts," whatever that means.

"A man gave me a plant," says Dottie, "a night-blooming cereus."

"Oh boy," says Judith.

"It's opening right now," says Dottie. "Five centimeters already."

"Very Georgia O'Keeffe," says Judith. They all explode with laughter.

The women are in their early to mid-sixties, and are recently retired. A lot of newer retirees tend to have more money than older retirees. It's a result of the economic boom of the nineties, which allowed newer retirees to sell their houses up North for a large profit. Bridgepoint, their community, is the nicest one I've ever seen. It's magnificent. There are no tall, Stalinist condominium buildings, like in Century Village. Large, stately, freestanding houses dot the community grounds, many of them abutting Bridgepoint's private golf course. It's a fantasyland for former executives, a whole other kind of retirement, and makes me wonder: Why have I been retiring in an old-person ghetto all this time when I could have been here? Artie and I could have been playing golf in style instead of on the lousy public course we always have to use. But to afford a place like this, I'd have to work myself silly for the next forty years.

"A canasta is seven cards," Judith tells me, after they begin to play. "You can use wilds. A canasta with wilds is dirty, without wilds is clean. Dirty is worth less than clean."

"Dirty canasta," repeats Dottie.

"But you can't start putting down canastas until you make your meld," says Judith. "That's also called your first lay."

"First lay!" says Dottie.

"You make a lay with at least three of a kind," says Judith. "Three through seven is worth five points, eight through king is worth ten points. Twos are wild, they're worth twenty points. Jokers are wild too. They're worth the most. Fifty points."

"You really want to get jokers," says Meredith. She starts to snicker. She turns to Dottie. "Tell him."

"Don't tell him," says Judith.

"I wasn't gonna tell him," says Dottie.

"Tell me what?" I have to ask.

"Nothing," says Judith.

"Tell you what we call jokers," says Meredith.

"We should tell him," says Dottie.

"Go ahead," says Judith. "You tell him. I'm not."

Dottie begins to laugh, then stops laughing, then laughs again, then stops.

"We have a special name for jokers," she says.

"What's that?" I ask.

"We call them Big Dicks!" says Dottie, and then she's off again, laughing, laughing, laughing!

"'Cause they're so hard to come by," explains Meredith.

Artie and I have been playing golf every few weeks, whenever Artie has a day off from work. I'm always happy when he calls. It's like Artie is the bad kid, and we're playing hooky from everything.

"All that career shit," he says, "too intense. Too much paranoia. You gotta get so stoned just to put it way back in the back of your head. If I had stayed here instead of going abroad, I woulda been eatin' my heart out." One morning, before golf, Artie has me meet him at his house in Fort Lauderdale. It's a small condo in a neat neighborhood. Towering over the development is a massive aqua blue water tower, which Artie tells me looks a lot like a chillum, an Indian hash pipe.

"That's funny," I say, "that you live here under the shadow of a giant hash pipe."

"How do you mean?" he says.

Artie introduces me to his dog, Bonzo, and his wife, Sandra. This is the first time I've met Sandra, and I have to admit that I'm surprised by how lovely and sweet she is. She looks years younger than her age, which is in the mid-fifties. Maybe heroin does keep you young. Sandra is busy making Artie an Orange Julius, which Artie tells me he drinks whenever he's taking methadone.

"I've heard a lot about you!" she says. "I hear you've been sponging up Artie's stories!"

We sit on the couch for a moment. Bonzo trots over and jumps up on me, licking my face.

"Down, Bonzo," says Artie, halfheartedly.

Artie tells me he's had bad luck with dogs in his life. This is his fifth dog in the last fifteen years.

"Wow," I say, "good thing you never had a kid."

"Oh," says Artie, "I have a kid. A son. First marriage."

"Great kid!" calls Sandra from the kitchen.

"Oh," I say, cringing a little. "That's cool."

"I didn't talk to him for fifteen years. Boy, was he pissed!"

"Yeah?"

"Pissed! He hated me! But we're cool now."

"Where does he live?"

"Atlanta. He's a musician! Very talented."

"Wow," I say, "that's awesome. You must be really proud."

"Oh yeah. Really proud," says Artie. He lowers his voice a bit. "He deals a little weed too."

"Yeah?" I say, and even though I know it's a dumb thing to add: "Like father like son, right?"

"Yeah!" says Artie. "I always say that about it!"

When I go to the swimming pool, a few days after my Bridgepoint canasta game, Shirley tells me that I'm welcome at her own game the following week. As I had hoped would happen, Shirley is a little jealous that I went to another canasta game, in the rich community no less.

"Will I be able to actually play in your game?" I ask.

"Why? Did they not let you play?"

"No," I say, "they let me play."

We sit there for a moment, as a jet flies overhead. Our swimming pool is under a flight path. Far above us the sun is glinting off the airplane's steel.

"How's Sunday?" she yells at me.

"Sunday's good!"

"Great! Make sure you call me on Saturday and see how I'm feeling, though. I'm supposed to have surgery on Monday!"

"You're having surgery?" I ask.

"Heart surgery," she says.

"Oh . . ." I say. "Isn't that . . . serious?"

"Ehhh," she says, "there's a fifty percent morbidity rate."

She says this to me like she's reporting the weather, or telling me her favorite cereal. This woman is having potentially fatal surgery on Monday. She might die. That is a pretty heavy thing just to mention by the pool. Don't we spend our whole lives, at bars and campfires, asking each other, "What would you do if this was your last day on earth?" Shirley has lots of friends and even relatives in the community. Why would she want to spend her last Sunday playing canasta with me? I don't want that kind of pressure. Being a woman's potential Last Sunday is worse than being a woman's first sexual partner, where if it goes lousy then, for the rest of her life, when she hears the phrase "bad sex," she thinks of you, or literally calls it "getting Rodneyed."

"That's okay," I say to Shirley. "It sounds like you might be busy. Why don't we play canasta some other time, after you recover?"

"Don't be silly," she says. "I don't want to make a big deal out of all that."

"But . . . aren't you scared?" I ask.

"Am I scared?" she says, repeating my words as if I have asked the dumbest question in the world. "Of course I'm scared. I'm terrified."

* * *

As Artie and I ride around in the golf cart, we shop for houses. Artie enjoys staring at the pricey Gold Coast homes ringing the course and imagining himself inside them. In our golf cart, he can almost drive right into the backyards of the nicer ones. He likes the ones with wraparound terraces. We both prefer the older ones, the beaten down homes with "character."

"You won't believe how much these ocean houses cost," says Artie. "They're fuckin' expensive." At one house, Artie takes out his cell phone and calls the number on the FOR SALE sign. I don't hear how much it costs, just a series of wordless noises on Artie's end, then he hangs up and doesn't mention it again.

"Why did you ever leave your life back overseas?" I ask him. I don't understand it.

"Look," he says, "my wife and I were shooting a thousand dollars a day apiece, four times a day. We'd party. People would come over, we'd turn 'em on. . . ."

Artie sighs. Basically, he explains, he was forced to come home. It turns out, he says, that taking heroin for thirty years isn't the best thing for your body. Sandra, in particular, wasn't doing too great after a while. She left for half a year to go live with her parents, and when she came back, Artie had to admit she looked a lot better. She talked him into coming home, moving close to her parents in Coconut Grove, and kicking the habit. Artie did that, then he relapsed. Then he kicked the habit again, then he relapsed again. A few years passed. He tried a few jobs but they didn't take. Eventually he drifted into real estate. He liked that he could make his own hours.

"Selling real estate is like selling dope. You're selling something. Someone wants it, you have it."

"Well," I say, "the profit margin is probably not quite so good."

"Yeah," he says, "I don't know. I'm still kind of trying to figure out what my thing is, you know?"

"I'm sure you could do lots of stuff," I say.

All of a sudden I'm giving career advice to a man who is almost old enough to be my grandfather. I'm thrown. I had always thought that old people had their thing figured out. I was banking on that, that whole *Morrie* fantasy. But now, after almost six months of living with elderly people, I know that you can bank on nothing. When you get older you are still the exact same person. You're not going to become wise or contented if you aren't wise or contented already. It reminds me of something Amy Ballinger said to me when we were at lunch once. I'd asked her if she thought that people get crankier when they get older—a question that a lot of my friends have been asking me ever since I got to Florida. Amy told me no.

"If they were nice when they were young, then they're nice when they die," she said. "Asshole when they were young, asshole dead."

At the time, I'd found that to be a depressing thought. But I think about it some more as Artie and I ride around the golf course, chasing down lost balls. It doesn't have to be depressing. There's something comforting about the idea that you're going to stay the same as you get older. It takes a lot of the pressure off. It saves you a lot of money spent on self-help books.

Artie takes the golf cart and pivots it up a small hill so we can look at a huge house with an inviting hammock. It's a stately, weathered old Colonial with a splintered wraparound terrace on both levels. It looks like the place Bob Marley would be living in if he were alive today. We sit there in front of the house for a few moments. It would be a great place to settle down when I'm finally ready for all that.

"Hey," he says, "from the second floor I bet you can see the ocean."

"Get your eyes off that house," I say. "That one's mine."

"In your dreams, kiddo," says Artie. "That one's mine."

* * *

On Sunday, I don't hear from Shirley about our canasta game, which is nothing new. I've accepted at this point that I am never going to actually play that game. Several days later I go to the pool. The Pool Group is sitting there, in a tight circle. I stand outside of it and don't say anything. I turn to Paula, the Pool Group gossip, and ask her if she's heard how Shirley's surgery went.

"She died," Paula says.

There are two women swimming laps in the pool. A jet plane is flying overhead. The sun is out.

"She died? From the surgery?" I say.

"It was very serious surgery," Paula says. "She was seventy-one."

Everyone is quiet. It occurs to me that I should have noticed that when I approached. I pull up a chair and sit down with them, saying nothing. I think to myself, *Good-bye, Shirley. You died nice.*

The Pool Group doesn't leave a seat open for Shirley. The circle of chairs is just closed a little tighter. I look around at all the women in the Pool Group, and the obvious dawns on me, that the circle is going to get tighter and tighter until I am the only one left. Who will I sit in a circle with then? It's the only important question. Why didn't I foresee the obvious structural flaw in my plan to test out retirement early? That all the new friends I make will be gone by the time I actually retire?

Neither Artie nor I feel like playing golf today. Instead, Artie suggests that we take his dog to the beach, which sounds ideal to me. At least once a day, Artie says, he drives the eight miles to the water and takes his dog to the beach.

"It's my favorite thing to do in Florida," he says. "As in, it's the only thing I like to do in Florida."

I throw the ball into the ocean and Bonzo swims in and

brings it back. The dog is a big dope, but lovable. After a few minutes, to keep things interesting, I start to heave the ball into the ocean so I can watch Bonzo work a little harder. Then Artie tells me not to throw the ball so far. "I don't want her eaten by a shark," he says.

"How great would it be to be a dog," I say, knowing Artie will agree with me.

"Oh yeah," he says. "Nothing to do all day but fuck around . . . people to take care of you . . ."

"I'm going home on Sunday," I tell him. "For a while . . ."

"Yeah," he says, "that's what I would do if I was you."

Even though Artie is a sixty-three-year-old former heroin addict with no idea what he wants to do with his life, it still feels great when he encourages me. He's good at it. I would recommend that anybody with a need for a father or mother figure spend six months testing out retirement early in Florida. There are millions of elderly people there in need of a child figure.

"You know what you should do with your life," I tell Artie. "You should be one of those cool guidance counselor guys."

"Nah," he says. "I'd miss 'the life' too much." Artie can pull off sentences like that. "I'm gonna give this a few more years. If it doesn't work out, then we'll move someplace cheap. Where the country is still in chaos. Maybe Mexico. I like that, someplace where it runs on baksheesh, you know?" By *baksheesh* Artie means bribes.

"And Sandra," he says, "Sandra can practice her tai chi there."

"Sounds like a plan," I say.

"Oh God," says Artie, "it better not be."

On my second-to-last night in town, I'm meeting Christina's parents. It seems like weird timing, but so is this whole trip. It needs to be done. I want to spend my last night in Florida with her in Miami Beach. We're not each other's *basherte,* but we have a great time together.

Christina prepares me for the encounter over the phone.

"Just so you know," she says, "my mom got a face-lift a few days ago, and her face still looks messed up, so don't act weird about it." After hearing that, I contemplate not going through with it at all. Somehow she has found a way to make meeting her parents even more freaky.

Christina answers the door and rolls her eyes at me.

"Sorry about this," she mouths.

I can already see her mother making her way toward the door from the back of the living room. The house is well kept, surrounded by plants, and quite dark. Her mother walks up to me and, as I notice that her face looks misshapen, I remember I'm not supposed to look at her face. Or rather: I'm supposed to look at her face, but I'm not supposed to look like I'm looking at her face. I try to do that.

"Hi," I say, "it's so great to meet you."

She shakes my hand and smiles at me. She's a pretty woman. She looks like an older version of Christina.

"We've heard a lot about you," she says. Everyone is saying what they are supposed to.

There is the low creak of footsteps from the other room, and I realize her father is approaching. I remind myself to shut up and deal. The good thing about Catholic Cuban fathers, I tell myself, is that they can be quite understanding about their only daughter having premarital sex with a commitment-phobe Jew.

The footsteps get louder, rumbling the floorboards, and her father emerges from one of the side hallways. He approaches me and, as he gets closer, I am delighted to discover that he is at least six inches shorter than me. Worst-case scenario, I could fall on him and pin him to the floor with my chest, and then all he would be able to muster is a feeble bite to my sternum with teeth softened by years of *café con leche* consumption.

"Rodney," he says to me, "how are you?" He smiles. His strong white teeth glisten against his brown skin.

"I'm great," I say. "How are you?"

"So Christina says you are from New York."

"Yes," I say. "I live in Los Angeles."

"You're a writer."

"Yes," I say.

"And what do you do down here?" he says.

He looks at me and smiles. I think about the question while my eyes dart around the room. On the wall behind him is a wooden crucifix. Jesus, cockblocking me to the bitter end. I look at Christina. She seems to shake her head at me, but I'm not sure. I look at her mother without looking at her, and then I look back at her father.

"I'm, uh . . . I'm, uh . . . I've been retired," I say.

Christina begins to laugh.

This morning I wake up in Century Village at 6 A.M. I'm going out for a final meal with Amy Ballinger. I step outside and walk around the community. There are a lot of people out already. I walk across the parking lot and say hi to everybody I recognize. Al is waxing his car at six-fifteen in the morning.

"How's it going?" I say.

"Hey fella," he says.

Amy's birthday will be her ninety-fourth. "I just keep going," she says. Then she adds an off-color joke, indicating that she may be old, but at least a couple of her appendages are still limber.

"Where are you going to now?" she asks me. I tell her I'm going back home to New York for Christmas, and then to Los Angeles to start working again.

"Are you going to call?" she asks.

"Yeah, I'm going to try to," I say.

"All the other old biddies down here, they all have kids, they get phone calls all the time."

"Uh . . . I'll definitely call."

"Okay," she says. "Good." Later, she wishes me best of luck writing about retirement "without boring everyone to tears."

"Thanks," I say.

In the condo, I pack up my stuff while my roommate, Margaret, plays piano in the living room. Ranchipurr and Petna begin to scratch on my door, and for the first time in months, I open the door and let them in to have the run of the place. It's their room again. They mind their own business and laze about on the floor. After I'm done packing I go outside to say goodbye to the birds. They fail to recognize the poignancy of the moment, and just repeat "Hey man, what's up, hey man, what's up" until I get annoyed and go back inside. The cats are in the same position I left them, but the three of us know that when I get home and open my suitcase, there will somehow be a steaming pile of cat feces nestled inside my folded sweaters.

The last thing I do is walk out to the swimming pool. It's already late afternoon, and the Pool Group is gone for the day. So I just leave my terry-cloth shirt out there on a chaise lounge as an offering, figuring that one of my friends will happen upon it and think: Hey . . . free terry.

Christina and I are on the beach at night, lying on a SpongeBob towel we bought in a drugstore. The lights of North Miami Beach stretch out behind us, and the ocean in front of us is a wall of black. Elderly people still live in this part of Miami Beach. They haven't been pushed out by pansexual nightclub promoters yet. I've been hearing that all over South Florida changes are starting to happen. Even at Century Village, condos left vacant by deceased retirees are being filled by younger Cubans and Haitians who have been moving north in large numbers ever since Hurricane Andrew.

Christina and I don't talk much. What is there to say? She says she's moving to Puerto Rico soon, and I'm going back home tomorrow to my actual life. This is the last peace I'll have for a while. My sister is getting married in a few days. It's going to be a lot of dancing, smiling, and listening to my parents' friends make derisive comments about Florida, even though they're getting up there in age and could do a whole lot worse than this place.

"Canasta is a Spanish game, you know," Christina says. "It means 'basket.' "

"You know how to play?" I say.

"Yeah. My relatives in Puerto Rico play it all the time."

"Can you teach me canasta tonight?" I say.

"No," she says. "Come back in forty years when you're old and look me up. Maybe then."

We sit there and watch the boats out on the ocean and the late-night planes flying up the coast and landing in Ft. Lauderdale. Tomorrow morning I will fly to New York for the wedding. Four weeks from now, I will fly back to Los Angeles and go back to work. As for canasta, I'm fine with waiting forty years. At least there will still be some mystery left when I move to Florida for good. But for now, I'm ready to come out of retirement and go home, and hopefully, sometime very soon, take a fucking vacation.

EPILOGUE

It's been three years since I left Century Village. Many of the people I wrote about are still around. Steven Goldman is still patrolling Boca Raton in a C.O.P. car. Artie is still playing golf, selling real estate, and listening to Radiohead. Hundreds of my fellow Century Village retirees showed up at my local Boca Raton *Early Bird* appearance. In that moment, I became one of the few people on earth who understands what it feels like to be Tom Jones. But Tom Jones probably isn't asked for advice on where to retire like I frequently am now. Apparently, I am now a retirement expert.

Amy Ballinger turned ninety-six this August. Other than some knee pain—okay, *a lot* of knee pain—she's as sharp as ever. When *The New York Times* interviewed Amy about the release of my book, she told them it "could have been funnier."

Later that week when the article was published, Amy called me to angrily complain that the Grey Lady had libeled her as a "foul-mouthed comedian." In the course of her harangue, she dropped at least three F-bombs.

Other people have left the community. Some have died: Norman, Mo, and surely others I haven't heard about. I hear the Pool Group doesn't meet much anymore. Vivian got married again, and, it must be said, did not agree with my characterization of our meetings. "That's not how I come on to people," she told me. Barbara Marks, who I helped out with Internet dating, went back north to be closer to family. Last year, my roommate Margaret moved to a new community as well. More than ever, Florida and Florida retirement is in strange transition. Newcomers move in, but the Newcomers Club is disbanded. Condos sit empty while the real-estate market skyrockets. In October 2005, Hurricane Wilma blew many of Century Village's roofs off. Christina brought her new boyfriend to my Miami book signing and asked me to sign her book in front of him. Twenty years from now, I wonder how much of the world I wrote about will still even exist.

More than anything, when I speak about the book, people want to know how living with older people "changed" me. Everyone is obsessed with redemption stories I suppose. I often make something up, but the truth is I wasn't so changed by the experience. Some mornings these days I wake up before work, weary, and think to myself: "Man, how crazy would it be to retire early instead of going to work today." For a moment, I actually forget I already wrote that book. But that's not to say I don't, in retrospect, treasure the experience of writing *Early Bird*. It gave me a chance to meet a lot of fascinating, kind people, and it gave me an excuse to listen to them tell stories. I genuinely made a lot of friends. I'm the only person I know my age who routinely gets voicemails and emails from old people I'm not related to.

People ask me if I was lonely living there in Century Village, with so few people my age. It occasionally was, I tell them, but most mornings, when I walked out my front door, I saw at least fifteen people I knew. My generation places such a great premium on privacy, on independence, on making enough money to have your own place. The retirement trend now is veering toward larger, stand-alone suburban-style homes in North Carolina and Arizona. We don't want to retire like our batty parents and grandparents did down in Ft. Lauderdale, right on top of one another, acting like high school students who happen to be eighty-three years old. We turned their plastic fruit and plastic sofa shields into a lighthearted joke. Three years ago, I got a book deal out of it. But since then I've come to understand how our grandparents got a lot right about retirement.

That's all for now. Thanks to everyone who has read *Early Bird,* and feel free to say hello. I can be reached through my website, rodneyrothman.com, or at rodneyrothman@gmail.com.

Yours,
Rodney Rothman
Los Angeles, March 2006

ACKNOWLEDGMENTS

I'd like to thank the many residents of Century Village and South Florida who graciously welcomed me into their lives. I am especially grateful to: Toni Gleeson and the women at Century Village Pembroke Pines, the Star Bakery, Amy Ballinger, the Breakfast Club, the Bullshit Club, the Shuffleboard Club, the Not for Women Only Club, the Art Appreciation Club, Delray Bingo, Sergeant Lindskoog, Lieutenant Stephen Goldman and the gang at the C.O.P. office off of Glades Rd., Al Caputo, Janice and Leon Cohen, Joel and Helen Dubin, Martha Freedberg and the good people at Lake Worth Gardens, Ari Fuhrman, Jo Galen, Allyn Greene, Bob Hover, Stuart Kaminsky, Diane Lade, Irwin Levy, Barbra Marks, Eli Mast, Minnie and the late, wonderful Norman Kleiman, Anthony Pinto, Lee Ravine, Gail Schwartz, Virginia Snider, Randy Van

Cleek, and many others who will recognize themselves in my book.

This book would not have been possible without the tireless editing (okay, hand-holding) of Geoff Kloske at Simon & Schuster; my literary agent, David McCormick; Tricia Wygal, the world's greatest production editor; my manager, David Miner; Tracey Guest, who handled publicity; my fact checker, Edith Honan; my patient television agent, Sue Naegle; and my researchers, Cindy Stabinsky and Will Reiser.

I'd also like to thank the many people who were kind enough to read early versions of the book and offer me their comments: Samantha, David, and Alexa Potack; Gretchen Anderson; Dan Saltzstein; Judd Apatow; Jon and Nell Beckerman; Greg Behrendt; Nick and Eva Bogaty; Dave Bry; Kelly Cole; John Colpitts; Will Dobson; Dave Eggers; Brent Forrester; Chris Harris and Hilary Liftin; Erinn Heilman; Mark Jordan; Ben Karlin; Peter Karp; Kerry Kohansky; Ali Rushfield; Jenn Ross; Eira Rojas; Inger Lund; Jill Leiderman; Jason Mantzoukas; Ryan Miller; Dan O'Brien; Jessica St. Clair; Robin Reiser; Brian Rosenworcel; Susan Shaffer; Stephen Sherrill; Nicholas Stoller and Francesca Delbanco; Sarah Vowell; Bill Wasik; Amy Weil; and Jason White.

I'd like to thank Jenni Konner, the first to encourage me to write this book.

John Gosen and Tony Aranella, the first to encourage me to write at all.

Most of all, my parents, Joan and Howard Rothman, who have been supportive and understanding throughout everything.

Last, I'd like to thank everyone who bought or borrowed this book. I'm assuming that the Pool Group bought just one copy and is passing it around.